PRINCETON STUDIES IN INTERNATIONAL FINANCE NO. 11

# Short-Term Capital Movements Under the Pre-1914 Gold Standard

### Arthur I. Bloomfield

INTERNATIONAL FINANCE SECTION
DEPARTMENT OF ECONOMICS
PRINCETON UNIVERSITY · 1963

PRINCETON STUDIES IN INTERNATIONAL FINANCE

◈

INTERNATIONAL FINANCE SECTION
DEPARTMENT OF ECONOMICS
PRINCETON UNIVERSITY

◈

1. MONETARY AND FOREIGN EXCHANGE POLICY IN ITALY,
BY FRIEDRICH A. AND VERA C. LUTZ

2. MULTIPLE EXCHANGE RATES AND ECONOMIC DEVELOPMENT,
BY EUGENE RICHARD SCHLESINGER

3. SPECULATIVE AND FLIGHT MOVEMENTS OF CAPITAL IN
POSTWAR INTERNATIONAL FINANCE,
BY ARTHUR I. BLOOMFIELD

4. POSTWAR BILATERAL PAYMENTS AGREEMENTS,
BY MERLYN NELSON TRUED AND RAYMOND F. MIKESELL

5. THE FIRST THREE YEARS OF THE SCHUMAN PLAN,
BY DEREK CURTIS BOK

6. NEGOTIATIONS FOR BENELUX:
AN ANNOTATED CHRONICLE, 1943-1956,
BY JAMES E. MEADE

7. THE IMPORT DEPENDENCE OF BRITAIN AND
WESTERN GERMANY: A COMPARATIVE STUDY,
BY H. H. LIESNER

8. FINANCING FREE WORLD TRADE
WITH THE SINO-SOVIET BLOC,
BY RAYMOND F. MIKESELL AND JACK N. BEHRMAN

9. THE UNITED STATES INVESTMENT GUARANTY PROGRAM
AND PRIVATE FOREIGN INVESTMENT,
BY MARINA VON NEUMANN WHITMAN

10. RESERVE-ASSET PREFERENCES OF CENTRAL BANKS AND
STABILITY OF THE GOLD-EXCHANGE STANDARD,
BY PETER B. KENEN

11. SHORT-TERM CAPITAL MOVEMENTS UNDER THE
PRE-1914 GOLD STANDARD,
BY ARTHUR I. BLOOMFIELD

PRINCETON STUDIES IN INTERNATIONAL FINANCE NO. 11

# Short-Term Capital Movements Under the Pre-1914 Gold Standard

Arthur I. Bloomfield

INTERNATIONAL FINANCE SECTION

DEPARTMENT OF ECONOMICS

PRINCETON UNIVERSITY

PRINCETON, NEW JERSEY

1963

Printed in the United States of America by Princeton University Press,
at Princeton, New Jersey

# PRINCETON STUDIES
## IN INTERNATIONAL FINANCE

THIS is the eleventh number in the series called PRINCETON STUDIES IN INTERNATIONAL FINANCE, published from time to time under the sponsorship of the International Finance Section of the Department of Economics at Princeton University. The author, Arthur I. Bloomfield, is Professor of Economics at the University of Pennsylvania and a third-time contributor to publications of the International Finance Section.

This series is intended to be restricted to meritorious research studies in the general field of international financial and economic problems, both policy and theory, which are too long for the journals and too short to warrant publication as books. The Section welcomes the submission of manuscripts for this series.

While the Section sponsors the STUDIES, the writers are free to develop their topics as they will. Their ideas and treatment may or may not be shared by the editorial committee of the Section or the members of the Department.

FRITZ MACHLUP
*Director*

*Princeton University*
*June 1963*

# TABLE OF CONTENTS

|  | Page |
|---|---|
| I. INTRODUCTION | 1 |
| | |
| II. OFFICIAL SHORT-TERM CAPITAL MOVEMENTS | 7 |
| Statistics of Official Foreign-Exchange Holdings | 7 |
| Official Holdings of Foreign Exchange and Gold | 14 |
| Official Foreign-Exchange Operations | 19 |
| Adequacy of International Monetary Reserves | 28 |
| | |
| III. PRIVATE SHORT-TERM CAPITAL MOVEMENTS | 34 |
| Kinds and Motivations | 34 |
| A Note on Statistics of Pre-1914 Private Short-term Capital Movements | 49 |
| The Scandinavian Countries | 50 |
| Canada | 62 |
| France | 65 |
| | |
| IV. INTERNATIONAL SHORT-TERM CREDITOR-DEBTOR POSITIONS | 71 |
| Great Britain | 71 |
| Other Countries | 77 |
| | |
| V. ABNORMAL MOVEMENTS OF SHORT-TERM CAPITAL | 83 |
| | |
| VI. CONCLUDING NOTE | 90 |
| Appendix I | 95 |
| Appendix II | 96 |
| Appendix III | 97 |

# LIST OF TABLES

*Page*

I. Reported Gross Official Holdings of Foreign-Exchange
Assets: End of 1913     8

II. Sign Correlations: Changes in Commercial-Bank Net
Foreign Assets and in Central-Bank Reserves,
Scandinavian Countries     58

III. Russian Short-Term Foreign Assets and Liabilities     80

# LIST OF CHARTS

1. Official Foreign Exchange Holdings     9

2, 3, 4. Major Components of Official Reserves     17, 18

5, 6. Gross Official Reserves (Gold and Foreign Exchange)
as a Percentage of Imports     31, 32

7, 8. Short-Term Foreign Assets of Commercial Banks and
Reserves of Central Bank     54, 55

9. Changes in Net (or Gross) Foreign Assets of Commercial Banks and in Reserves of Central Bank     57

10. Canada: "Outside Reserves" of the Chartered Banks     64

11. France: Foreign Bill Holdings of Commercial Banks
and Net Gold Imports     69

# I. INTRODUCTION

Not since the international financial upheavals of the nineteen thirties have short-term capital movements attracted as much attention or provoked as much discussion as they have during the past few years. International transfers of short-term funds have increased markedly in volume and volatility since the restoration of currency convertibility by the leading countries of Western Europe at the end of 1958. Changing interest-rate differentials and forward-exchange rates between financial centers, expectations of exchange-rate adjustments, political uncertainties, and other factors have prompted sudden and substantial shifts of liquid funds across national boundaries that have at times had major disequilibrating effects upon the balances of payments of the countries concerned. These movements have also added to the difficulties of the monetary authorities in their efforts to maintain domestic economic stability and have complicated the problem of harmonizing internal and external objectives of financial policy. In some circles there are fears concerning the possibility of precipitate liquidations of the huge foreign short-term liabilities of the two reserve centers, the United States and the United Kingdom—to say nothing of outflows of domestic short-term funds—on a scale that could put such heavy pressures on their official reserves as to seriously undermine the foundations of the international monetary system. Recognition of the disturbances and dangers inherent in sudden and erratic movements of short-term funds from center to center and the large-scale conversion of reserve currencies into gold has resulted during the past few years in the adoption of a variety of national and international measures and the elaboration of a number of plans to counteract such movements and to strengthen the world's payments mechanism against these and other potential shocks.[1]

[1] This study is an outgrowth of research undertaken in Europe in 1957-8 under a year's grant from the Rockefeller Foundation. Acknowledgment is also made of a summer grant in 1961 from the National Science Foundation through the University of Pennsylvania. Thanks are also due to those many foreign central bankers, commercial bankers, and government officials who helped me in the collection or interpretation of statistical and other data relating to their respective countries. In drafting this paper I have been helped in a variety of ways by my former colleague, Dr. F. H. Klopstock of the Federal Reserve Bank of New York. On certain statistical details I have benefited from the advice of Professors M. Hamburg, L. R. Klein, and R. Summers of the University of Pennsylvania. I alone am responsible for any errors of fact or shortcomings of logic contained in this study. The charts were drawn by Mr. John H. Hendrickson.

In current discussions of international monetary organization and reform, nostalgic reference is sometimes made to the "good old days" of the international gold standard from 1880 to 1914 when these and other related problems now facing monetary authorities are supposed to have been of little importance or even nonexistent. Thus, for example, it is often stated or implied that in those days "hot-money" movements were almost unheard of, short-term capital flows were almost invariably equilibrating in character, short-term foreign indebtedness and the level of international reserves were matters of little concern, and so forth. Yet in actual fact many of the international financial problems of today were by no means without their parallels in the years before World War I, even if admittedly they were of considerably less importance. Disequilibrating movements of short-term capital, destabilizing exchange speculation, capital flight, threats to the continued maintenance of convertibility, concern as to the adequacy of international reserves and the volume of floating international indebtedness—all these at times were in evidence under the pre-1914 system and in some cases necessitated measures going well beyond routine application of discount-rate policy.

The fact is that we still know far too little about the actual functioning of the pre-1914 gold standard, which was a much more complex mechanism than is often believed, and are prone to rely far too much on oversimplifications and stereotypes as a substitute for detailed empirical research. In an earlier study I explored one of the many neglected areas of research in this field, by a comparative examination of the monetary policies of European central banks from 1880 to 1914, and cast some doubt upon the validity of various generally accepted views as to the nature and role of these policies.[2] An attempt will be made in the present study to throw some further light upon another aspect of the pre-1914 system by assembling and analyzing for a variety of countries some quantitative data and other material relating to short-term capital movements that have not as yet been systematically put together and evaluated. While the primary focus will be on international transfers of short-term funds—mainly between gold-standard countries—attention will also be given to some related matters such as international liquidity and gold-exchange-standard arrangements before 1914.

Published statistics relating to short-term capital movements before

[2] A. I. Bloomfield, *Monetary Policy under the International Gold Standard, 1880-1914* (New York, 1959).

1914, at least so far as *private* movements are concerned, are exceedingly hard to come by. This is not at all surprising when one realizes how inadequate such statistics are even today for the great majority of countries. One writer could cite only two countries before World War I (Sweden and Finland) for which the short-term foreign assets and liabilities of the commercial banks were regularly published.[3] Those economists who have constructed annual balance-of-payments statements for individual countries before 1914 have in nearly all cases had to include short-term capital movements (or the private component thereof) in a residual item along with long-term capital movements and/or errors and omissions. In view of this scarcity of data, it is understandable why previous attempts statistically to analyze various aspects of the behavior of short-term capital movements before 1914, notably those of Neisser[4] and Morgenstern,[5] have chosen to approach the problem indirectly, and to draw inferences as to the pattern of these movements, by using related financial series such as interest-rate differentials and exchange rates between pairs of countries, international gold movements, etc.

While pre-1914 statistics relating to private short-term capital movements are seriously deficient, no one has as yet attempted to assemble and analyze such series as are available. In actual fact, moreover, the amount of published data in this field is somewhat larger than is generally believed, even if most of it relates to smaller gold-standard countries. In a few cases I have also been able to construct series from the unpublished records of leading commercial banks in the countries concerned. Admittedly, these various series are all subject to distinct limitations from an analytical viewpoint, but they seem to be of sufficient interest to justify examination.

Statistics relating to *official* movements of short-term funds before 1914 are, on the other hand, reasonably good, although these have never been systematically put together. The majority of central banks that held foreign short-term assets usually reported them separately on their balance sheets, or at least that part of them that constituted legal cover

[3] F. G. Conolly, "Memorandum on the International Short-term Indebtedness," *The Improvement of Commercial Relations Between Nations and the Problems of Monetary Stabilization* (Paris, 1936), p. 353.

[4] H. Neisser, "Der Internationale Geldmarkt vor und nach dem Kriege," *Weltwirtschaftliches Archiv*, April 1929, pp. 171-226, and July 1930, pp. 150-202.

[5] O. Morgenstern, *International Financial Transactions and Business Cycles* (Princeton, 1959). On page 164, Morgenstern refers to "the annoying lack of statistics on short-term capital movements [before 1914]."

against central-bank note and deposit liabilities. In some cases, too, the foreign short-term assets held separately by treasuries and other official institutions were also published. Where statistics of central-bank and treasury holdings were not published in one form or another, I was able in some of these cases to get them directly from the institutions concerned.

This study avoids duplicating the much more ambitious statistical undertakings of Morgenstern and Neisser, which in any case have a somewhat different focus and are limited to the four leading gold-standard countries; and it deals with certain aspects of the subject with which they were not directly concerned. Its main purpose, as already suggested, is to present a variety of statistics and related materials on pre-1914 short-term capital movements and to draw such limited conclusions as the data permit.

The span of the international gold standard, stretching from about 1880 to 1914, was a relatively brief one. In 1880 the following were the main countries on the gold standard or some variant thereof: Great Britain, France, Germany, the United States, Belgium, Holland, Switzerland, Norway, Sweden, Denmark, Finland, Canada, Australia, South Africa, and New Zealand. They were joined in 1890 by Roumania, at the turn of the century by Russia, Japan, India, Argentina, Italy, and Austria-Hungary,[6] and in the early years of the 20th century by a number of other Asiatic and Latin American countries. Exchange rates between gold-standard countries were maintained within narrow limits approximating their respective gold points, without the support of exchange restrictions, direct import controls, or any significant degree of international monetary cooperation. Only a trifling number of countries were forced off the gold standard, once adopted. Other countries, including Spain, Greece, China, and various Latin American and Asiatic countries, remained throughout the period on a fluctuating-paper or silver-standard basis.

The form of the gold standard, both in its external and internal manifestations, revealed an almost bewildering diversity of legal and institutional arrangements from country to country. Some countries were on a full gold standard, others on a limping standard, and still others on a form of gold-exchange standard. Gold coin formed a rela-

---

[6] Italy and Austria-Hungary did not *legally* go on to the gold standard at all, but from the turn of the century kept their exchange rates relatively stable in terms of gold currencies and close to their own theoretical gold parities. Italy had actually gone legally on to the gold standard as early as 1881, but had abandoned it in 1891.

tively substantial part of the circulating medium in some countries, but a negligible part in most. Central banking was confined almost entirely to Europe; elsewhere in the gold-standard world the task of "managing" the standard was left to treasuries, other official institutions, or the commercial banks themselves. Money markets, where they existed at all, were in differing stages of development and linked together with differing degrees of cohesion. Despite these and many other diversities, all of the members of the gold-standard "club" had the common policy objective of seeking to maintain the convertibility of their currencies directly or indirectly into gold at the legal parity.[7]

According to the usual definition, an outflow of short-term capital from a given country involves an increase in its short-term claims on foreigners (nonresidents) and/or a decrease in foreign-owned short-term claims on that country. Conversely, an inflow of short-term capital into a country involves a decrease in its short-term claims on foreigners and/or an increase in foreign-owned short-term claims on that country. A short-term claim (asset) is defined in this connection as one with an original maturity of less than one year, including of course deposits and currency. Long-term capital movements involve changes in assets with an original maturity of more than one year as well as in holdings of shares of stock, real property, etc. This criterion for distinguishing short-term and long-term capital movements does not, of course, indicate whether or not a given capital movement is likely to be temporary and reversed within a short time. Indeed, a short-term capital movement as defined above could be "long-term" from the viewpoint of *motivation,* or conversely. But the asset basis of classification has at least the advantage of being objectively identifiable, and will be adhered to here; where exceptions are made they will be noted. For this reason, this study will not deal with international movements of outstanding (long-term) securities, although these are often motivated by the same factors influencing short-term capital transfers, and are known to have been very important in the pre-1914 period.[8]

For purposes of exposition we may also distinguish "official" and "private" short-term capital movements. An official short-term capital movement may be defined as one involving a change in short-term

---

[7] For more details on these matters, see part II of the study cited in footnote 2 above.

[8] For an analysis of these movements, with some historical material, see my paper "The Significance of Outstanding Securities in the International Movement of Capital," *Canadian Journal of Economics and Political Science,* November 1940, pp. 495-524. See also Morgenstern, *op.cit.,* pp. 507-528.

claims on foreigners held by official institutions of a given country, notably central banks and treasuries, regardless of whether or not the foreigners concerned are themselves official institutions. Likewise, a private short-term capital movement will be defined as one involving a change in short-term claims on foreigners held by private institutions, firms, or individuals of a given country, regardless of whether or not the foreigners concerned are themselves private parties. In short, we base the distinction between these two categories of short-term capital movements on the official or private character of the *owners* of the claims on foreigners, not that of the foreigners on whom the claims are held. In actual practice one can not always determine precisely whether a given owner of foreign short-term claims is in the "official" or "private" category. Moreover, both official and private short-term capital movements frequently perform in effect an identical role in the balance of payments. Nevertheless, these two broad classes of movements are sufficiently distinct as to motivations to justify their separate treatment here. But the interrelations between the two will also be examined.

## II. OFFICIAL SHORT-TERM CAPITAL MOVEMENTS

With the notable exception of the Bank of England, nearly all central banks during all or part of the period 1880-1914 held some foreign-exchange assets[1] in addition to gold in their international monetary reserves. These holdings, apart from earning interest (unlike gold), enabled central banks to intervene directly in the exchange market when it was desired to keep or to influence exchange rates within the gold points. Central-bank legal minimum-reserve requirements usually provided that foreign-exchange assets or specified categories thereof could be included in the legal cover up to a maximum amount or maximum proportion of the total cover, and in some cases in unlimited amounts.

In a number of countries, even some with central banks, national treasuries or other official agencies also held some foreign exchange on their own account, whether for purposes of stabilizing exchange rates or meeting external debt service or other official expenditures abroad, or as a reflection of temporarily unutilized proceeds of borrowings on foreign markets. In countries where central banks existed, however, any foreign balances held by the government were usually held through the intermediary of the central bank or merged completely with the latter's own holdings.

*Statistics of Official Foreign-Exchange Holdings*

Table I brings together statistics of reported official holdings of foreign-exchange assets by individual countries at the end of 1913, converted into dollars on the basis of the existing rates of exchange and broken down according to central-bank and other official holders. The total of such assets, which is believed to be reasonably complete, amounted to $963 million, over half of which was represented by the holdings of three countries: Russia, India, and Japan. This figure compares with total official gold holdings on the same date of about $4.9 billion for all countries,[2] including those that held no official foreign-exchange assets. Clearly, from the viewpoint of the world as a whole,

[1] In the discussion that follows, the terms "foreign-exchange assets," "foreign exchange," "foreign balances," and "foreign short-term assets" will be used interchangeably.

[2] Board of Governors of the Federal Reserve System, *Banking and Monetary Statistics* (Washington, 1943), p. 544.

foreign exchange was a smaller fraction of total official monetary reserves in 1913 than it has been in more recent years.

TABLE I

Reported Gross Official Holdings of
Foreign-Exchange Assets: End of 1913[a]
(millions of 1913 dollars[b])

| Country | Central Bank | Treasury or Other Official Agencies | Total |
|---------|--------------|-------------------------------------|-------|
| Russia | 86.2 | 219.9 | 306.1 |
| India | | 136.4 | 136.4 |
| Japan | | 115.8[c] | 115.8 |
| Belgium | 32.2 | 45.5[d] | 77.7 |
| Italy | 38.1[e] | 13.5[f] | 51.6 |
| Germany | 49.6 | | 49.6 |
| Greece | 43.7[g] | | 43.7 |
| Sweden | 34.3 | 9.1[h] | 43.4 |
| Chile | | 39.0 | 39.0 |
| Finland | 20.9 | | 20.9 |
| Austria-Hungary | 12.2 | | 12.2 |
| Philippines | | 11.4[i] | 11.4 |
| Roumania | 10.9 | | 10.9 |
| Norway | 8.9 | | 8.9 |
| Switzerland | 8.2 | | 8.2 |
| Denmark | 6.2 | | 6.2 |
| Netherlands | 5.5 | | 5.5 |
| Ceylon | | 4.9 | 4.9 |
| Java | 4.7 | | 4.7 |
| France | 3.2 | | 3.2 |
| Bulgaria | 2.7 | | 2.7 |
| TOTAL | 367.5 | 595.5 | 963.0 |

[a] For sources, see Appendix III.

[b] For exchange rates in terms of the dollar in 1913 (and during the gold-standard period as a whole), see Appendix I.

[c] Yokohama Specie Bank. No statistics are available regarding the foreign-exchange assets of the Bank of Japan and the Japanese Government.

[d] Belgian Government ($13.7 million) and *Caisse Générale d'Epargne et de Retraite* ($31.8 million).

[e] Three Italian Banks of Issue.

[f] June 30 figure.

[g] Includes a small amount of gold that cannot be separated out.

[h] Swedish National Debt Office.

[i] December 31, 1911. Later figures are not available.

Chart 1 brings together, for the first time to my knowledge, year-end statistics of aggregate official foreign-exchange holdings from 1880 to 1913, broken down according to the individual countries concerned.[3]

[3] The underlying statistics are given in Appendix II and the sources in Appendix III.

8

CHART 1

## OFFICIAL FOREIGN EXCHANGE HOLDINGS

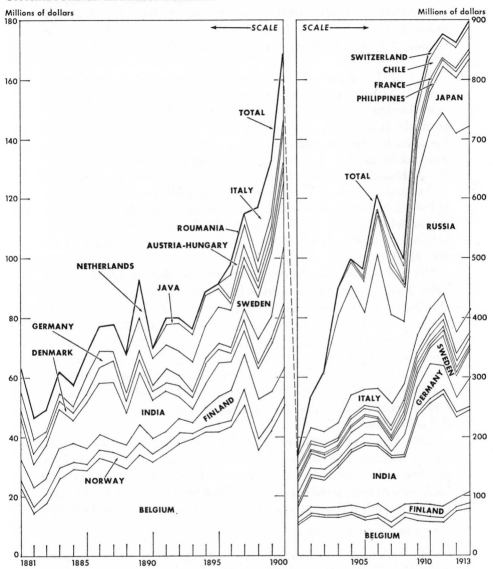

Millions of dollars

180

160

140

120

100

80

60

40

20

0

←—SCALE

TOTAL

ITALY

ROUMANIA

AUSTRIA-HUNGARY

NETHERLANDS

JAVA

SWEDEN

GERMANY

DENMARK

INDIA

FINLAND

NORWAY

BELGIUM

1881    1885    1890    1895    1900

Millions of dollars

900

800

700

600

500

400

300

200

100

0

SCALE—→

SWITZERLAND

CHILE

FRANCE

PHILIPPINES    JAPAN

TOTAL

RUSSIA

ITALY

SWEDEN

GERMANY

INDIA

FINLAND

BELGIUM

1905    1910    1913

Note: Figures converted into dollars on basis of pre-1914 rates of exchange.

9

All of the figures have been converted into dollars on the basis of pre-1914 exchange rates.[4] In view of the very sharp increase in the aggregate of these assets after 1900, it was necessary to break the chart into two sections, each with a different scale. The individual lines at the beginning of the second section correspond to those at the end of the first.

Most of the individual series begin later than 1880, usually in the year in which the official institutions concerned actually began to acquire foreign exchange and/or for which the relevant data become available. In a few cases, notably Russia, Austria-Hungary, and Italy, the series in question could have been started a few years earlier but were not because, due to fluctuating exchange rates in those years for the currencies concerned, I was unable to determine what rates of exchange should be used to convert the reported local-currency amounts of the official foreign balances into dollars,[5] i.e., what rates of exchange the official institutions involved had originally used in converting their holdings of foreign balances into local-currency equivalents for balance-sheet purposes.

The statistics of official foreign-exchange holdings in Chart 1 (and Table I) are presented on a gross basis and not on a net basis after allowance for the short-term foreign liabilities, if any, of the institutions concerned. As it so happens, statistics of such liabilities are available for only a few countries, e.g., Sweden, Finland and Italy, and the amounts involved were relatively small. Foreign *bonds* have been included in official foreign balances in those few instances where separate figures were available, e.g., Sweden, Japan and Finland, although technically speaking they do not constitute foreign short-term assets as defined earlier.[6]

While the identification of "official institutions" whose foreign-exchange holdings were to be included in the series generally posed no problem, a few borderline cases presented themselves where central banks or treasuries were not involved. Most prominent was the Belgian *Caisse Générale d'Epargne et de Retraite*, a government-owned savings

[4] For the rates of exchange used here and elsewhere in this study, see Appendix I.

[5] The series for Russia, Austria-Hungary, and Italy could actually have been started in 1893, 1886, and 1894, respectively. Although the ruble was stabilized in terms of gold in 1897, the Russian series does not start until 1901 because statistics of the foreign-exchange holdings of the Russian Government (as contrasted with the State Bank) are not available before that year.

[6] Central-bank balance sheets usually classified foreign assets according to foreign bills and sums due from foreign correspondents.

bank that held substantial foreign short-term assets but which has generally been included by Belgian statisticians in the private sector. It was decided to include these assets in the Belgian series, not merely because the *Caisse* was publicly owned, but more especially because it sometimes made part of its foreign exchange available to the National Bank of Belgium in case of need.[7] In the case of Italy the decision was made to include the foreign-exchange assets not only of the Bank of Italy but also of the Bank of Naples and the Bank of Sicily, which continued to issue notes after the Bank of Italy's establishment in 1893. This was done, in keeping with the procedure of Italian statisticians, on the ground that these two institutions were considered at that time to be as "official" as the Bank of Italy itself, and because there were no differences in the rights and obligations of all three banks. Less troublesome were the cases of the Yokohama Specie Bank, a government-owned institution established in 1880 that conducted all foreign-exchange operations on behalf of the Japanese authorities, and the Swedish National Debt Office, which conducted overseas borrowing operations on behalf of the government and which on a number of occasions lent some of its foreign balances to the Bank of Sweden. The overseas balances of these two institutions were included in the respective series.

Some of the series of official foreign balances in Chart 1 doubtless understate to some degree the actual totals. In the case of Japan, for example, it is known that the central bank and the government held some foreign-exchange assets apart from those held by the Yokohama Specie Bank. From 1903 to 1913 there is available an official year-end series of "gold held abroad" jointly by these two authorities, the annual totals ranging from $9.4 million to $220.7 million.[8] The Bank of Japan has informed me that, while the bulk of this item represented actual gold held under earmark abroad, an indeterminable part consisted of holdings of bank deposits abroad and foreign treasury bills. In the absence of a statistical breakdown, no allowance could be made for such holdings in our Japanese series, which is confined to the Yokohama Specie Bank alone.[9]

[7] P. Kauch, *La Banque Nationale de Belgique* (Brussels, 1950), pp. 247-248 and *passim*.

[8] This series is reproduced in H. G. Moulton, *Japan* (Washington, 1931), p. 412, and in H. Shinjo, *History of the Yen* (Kobe, 1962), p. 103.

[9] Although our Japanese series starts only in 1903, it is known that the Japanese authorities had begun to acquire large balances in London as early as 1895 as a result of the receipt in sterling of the Chinese war indemnity following the Sino-Japanese war of 1894-1895. That indemnity, amounting to a total of about £ 38

The total is also understated somewhat in the case of Austria-Hungary. The Austro-Hungarian Bank reported separately on its balance sheet only that foreign exchange which could be included in its legal-reserve cover, namely, any amount up to 60 million crown ($12.2 million). After 1900 its reported holdings of foreign exchange remained unchanged at that figure, although its actual holdings are believed to have been much larger.[10] It is possible that a few of the other central banks included in our series may have also understated to some degree their actual holdings.

The Italian figures are understated in view of the fact that no allowance has been made for the foreign-exchange holdings of the Italian Treasury, statistics for which were available only on a June 30 basis. Between 1898 and 1913 these holdings ranged from $5.6 million to $24.3 million, as compared with a range of $17.9 million to $38.1 million for the year-end holdings of the three issue banks which are plotted on the chart.

Certain central banks that are known to have held foreign exchange could not be included because the necessary statistics were lacking (e.g., the National Bank of Greece[11] and the National Bank of Bulgaria). The holdings of certain national treasuries and government agencies had to be excluded for the same reason. It is not believed, however, that these omissions were very serious. In certain cases where the necessary figures were available, they were not included in Chart

---

million ($190 million), was paid in instalments in London over a three-year period. See M. Matsukata, *Report on the Adoption of the Gold Standard in Japan* (Tokyo, 1899), pp. 166-173.

[10] The Bank for International Settlements, for example, estimated that between 1903 and 1913 the actual total ranged between 60-150 million crown ($12.2-$30.5 million). *The Gold Exchange Standard*, mimeographed (Basle, 1932), p. 3. It may be significant that the item "*Sonstige Aktiva*" on the Austro-Hungarian Bank's balance sheet, in which these unreported holdings are believed to have been included, rose sharply and behaved highly erratically after 1900.

[11] Statistics of the "foreign-exchange" holdings of the National Bank of Greece are available for many years before 1913, but they include an unspecified amount of gold. In any case, conversion of these figures into dollars was impossible because of fluctuating rates of exchange for the drachma during most of the earlier years and because of lack of information as to those rates and the accounting practices of the Bank.

The League of Nations, in its *Memorandum on Currency and Central Banks, 1913-1925*, Vol. II (Geneva, 1926), gives a figure of 194 million pesetas as the amount of "foreign balances and bills" held by the Bank of Spain at the end of 1913. The Bank of Spain has informed me that the League was in error, and that the item in question, available also for earlier years, consisted predominantly of gold held under earmark abroad.

1 because the amounts involved were trifling (for example, Ceylon and Uruguay[12]).

As against these various factors tending to understate the totals of official foreign balances, there is the probability that the Russian figures may to some degree overstate them. The reported assets held abroad by the State Bank of Russia and the Russian Government, which we have assumed for purposes of Chart 1 to consist entirely of foreign-exchange assets, may well have included a certain amount of gold held under earmark abroad. It has been impossible to get precise information on this point, but all available evidence suggests that the earmarked gold component was relatively small. Even so, our assumption may involve a considerable overstatement in absolute terms of the total amount of official foreign-exchange assets in view of the huge size of Russia's reported official assets abroad.

Whatever the limitations of the series as described above, there can be no doubt about the sharp increase that took place in the aggregate of official foreign balances over the period 1880 to 1913 as a whole. An inspection of Chart 1 reveals that from 1880 to 1899 the total rose moderately from about $60 million to $130 million, but that thereafter it increased by almost eight-fold to approximately $1 billion at the end of 1913.[13] This accelerated rate of growth was attributable almost entirely to the accumulation of official Russian and Japanese balances at the turn of the century and their rapid increase thereafter, and to the sharp rise in Indian balances. Official institutions in a number of other countries also began to hold foreign exchange after 1900, but the amounts involved did not appreciably add to the totals.

Little concrete information is available as to the countries on which official foreign short-term claims were held. Central banks and treasuries occasionally listed the various centers in which their overseas balances were held—usually a wide and diversified list[14]—but only rarely, and then only for isolated dates, was a statistical breakdown by coun-

[12] For Ceylon, see B. R. Shenoy, *Ceylon Currency and Banking* (London, 1941), pp. 248-253. For Uruguay, see *Banco de la Republica Oriental del Uruguay, 1896-1917* (Montevideo, 1918), p. 337.

[13] The actual total shown in Chart 1 is $898 million, as compared with the figure of $963 million given in Table I. The difference between the two reflects the fact that the foreign exchange of the Greek and Bulgarian central banks and of the Italian Treasury are not included in Chart 1, for reasons explained in the text, but are included in Table I.

[14] For example, the State Bank of Russia listed Berlin, Paris, London, Vienna, Brussels, Hamburg, Amsterdam, Copenhagen, Stockholm, Milan, and Basle. See E. Slansky, *La Banque Impériale de Russie* (St. Petersburg, 1910), p. 96.

tries provided. In view of the dominant position of Great Britain in world trade and finance and the unquestioned convertibility of the pound into gold, a very large proportion of the aggregate of official foreign-exchange holdings at any time undoubtedly consisted of sterling bills, deposits in London banks, and other short-term sterling assets. For example, all of the Indian balances were in sterling and the bulk of the Japanese holdings are also believed to have been in that form. The picture is less clear with regard to official Russian balances, especially in view of their frequent shifting from center to center. While Russian balances in London were at times relatively substantial,[15] it is likely that the amounts held in Paris were customarily larger in view of the particularly close financial ties between Russia and France. Out of a total of 594 million rubles ($306 million) of official Russian foreign-exchange holdings on January 1, 1914—probably a quite unrepresentative date but the only one for which I have a breakdown—as much as 431 million rubles were claims on France, as compared with only 46 million on England, 103 million on Germany, and 14 million on other countries.[16] As for the smaller holders of official foreign-exchange assets, the sums involved were undoubtedly divided mainly between England, France and Germany. It is not believed that any relatively substantial amount of these assets represented claims on the United States.[17]

## Official Holdings of Foreign Exchange and Gold

To determine the relative contribution of official foreign-exchange holdings to the growth in the world's aggregate stock of official international monetary reserves from 1880 to 1914, it would of course be necessary to compare the totals in Chart 1 with the increase in total official gold reserves during the same period, including those of coun-

[15] It is believed that the balances in London of the Russian Government alone amounted at one time to £20 million (roughly $100 million). See T. Balogh, *Studies in Financial Organization* (Cambridge, 1947), p. 183.

[16] V. A. Mukoseyev, "Money and Credit," in *Russia: Its Trade and Commerce*, ed. by A. Raffalovich (London, 1918), pp. 398-399. One writer has stated that in normal times about 60 per cent of official Russian balances were deposited with French banks. See O. Crisp, "French Investments in Russian Joint-Stock Companies, 1894-1914," *Business History*, June 1960, p. 90n.

[17] The small foreign balances of the Philippine Treasury were held entirely in the United States and those of the Bank of Java mainly in Holland. The balances of the Chilean Treasury are believed to have been held mainly in London. In the case of the Bank of Finland, for which the relevant statistics for various dates were made available to me, Germany proved consistently to be the largest single creditor. Germany's own foreign-exchange holdings were mainly in the form of sterling.

tries which held no official foreign exchange.[18] Unfortunately, no series for total official gold holdings before 1914 are readily available. Indeed, the only detailed estimate of which I am aware is for December 31, 1913, which gives a total of $4.9 billion.[19] Estimates for earlier years, available only for scattered dates, are not only incomplete but also include gold held by banks that were not in the "official" category. For our purpose, however, "corrected" estimates for merely a few of the earlier years will suffice. An extremely rough estimate for 1880 that I have made on the basis of a tabulation by the U.S. Bureau of the Mint,[20] adjusted and supplemented where possible, yields a figure of about $1 billion. A much more complete tabulation for December 31, 1903 by the U.S. Comptroller of the Currency,[21] which I have again adjusted where necessary, indicates a total of approximately $2.6 billion.

A comparison of these estimates of total official gold reserves for 1880, 1903, and 1913 with those of official foreign-exchange holdings for the same dates yields the following results. Over the period as a whole the former rose by about $3,900 million, as compared with an increase for the latter of only about $900 million.[22] Between 1903 and 1913 alone, official gold reserves rose by $2,300 million, whereas official foreign exchange increased by some $500 million. Clearly the great bulk of the growth in official monetary reserves between 1880 and 1913 was provided by gold. World gold production had been greatly stepped up after 1890 with the discovery of new gold mines in South Africa and America and of new technical processes for working old mines.[23] Although a substantial part of the increased output was diverted into industry and the arts, into private hoards in India and elsewhere, and into internal monetary circulation, more than half found its way into official hands.

In the absence of more adequate global statistics of official gold reserves before 1914, some further light may be thrown on the relative

[18] The most notable examples of such countries were the United States and Great Britain.

[19] See footnote 2, p. 7.

[20] *Annual Report of the Director of the Mint* (Washington, 1881), p. 114.

[21] *Annual Report of the Comptroller of the Currency* (Washington, 1904), Vol. I, p. 402.

[22] The figure of $900 million was obtained by subtracting aggregate official foreign-exchange holdings at the end of 1880 ($63 million) from the 1913 total given in Table I ($963 million).

[23] The annual average of world gold production rose from 5.1 million ounces ($105.4 million) in 1881-1890 to 10.2 million ounces ($210.8 million) in 1891-1900 and to 18.3 million ounces ($378.3 million) in 1901-1910. See C. O. Hardy, *Is There Enough Gold?* (Washington, 1936), p. 42.

movements of official gold and exchange holdings by examining the behavior of these two components of monetary reserves for those individual countries that held official foreign balances. Charts 2, 3, and 4 plot the relevant data on a year-end basis for most of the countries included in Chart 1, all of the figures being converted into dollars on the basis of the existing rates of exchange. The three charts are drawn on different scales to accommodate the widely differing levels of reserves in various groups of the countries concerned.[24] Official (central-bank) holdings of silver are also shown in those cases where such holdings were of significant size in relation to gold and foreign exchange. To be sure, silver did not have the same status from the viewpoint of settling international balances, but it did constitute an official asset that could be sold abroad at whatever price it would fetch[25] in case of need. Indeed, for Belgium, Switzerland, and Italy domestic silver coin was accepted at par in France under the terms of the Latin Monetary Union,[26] and official holdings of such coin were thus the virtual equivalent of gold or gold exchange.[27]

Charts 2, 3, and 4, apart from what they indicate about the differences in the absolute size of monetary reserves from country to country, reveal a variety of patterns with respect to the relative levels and movements of official gold and foreign-exchange holdings in each. In most of the countries gold reserves were consistently larger and in some cases very much larger than holdings of foreign exchange, the only exceptions being India, Finland, Sweden, and Belgium. In nearly all instances gold reserves rose in absolute terms more than foreign exchange over the period as a whole, except for Finland, Belgium, and

[24] The statistics of official foreign-exchange holdings used in the three charts are identical with those underlying Chart 1. In the case of Italy, however, the foreign exchange of the Italian Treasury, which was excluded from Chart 1, is shown separately (on a June 30 basis) in Chart 3. The various gold series were taken from central-bank statements or, as in the case of Japan and India, from other official sources mentioned in the text or Appendix III. The French and German gold figures are annual averages of monthly figures rather than year-end data. Some of the other governments may have held independent gold reserves, but the necessary data are not available.

[25] Between 1880 and 1913 the world price of silver in terms of gold fell by approximately 50 per cent. There is reason to believe that the silver holdings shown in the charts, which were taken from central-bank statements, are overstated in terms of their actual market values in at least some of the cases.

[26] These countries granted reciprocal privileges to France and to each other.

[27] From the viewpoint of *internal* convertibility, with which we are not concerned here, silver holdings were also important for those central banks that chose to redeem their currencies in silver for purposes of internal circulation or in countries where the public preferred silver to gold coin as a circulating medium.

*16*

CHART 2

## MAJOR COMPONENTS OF OFFICIAL RESERVES

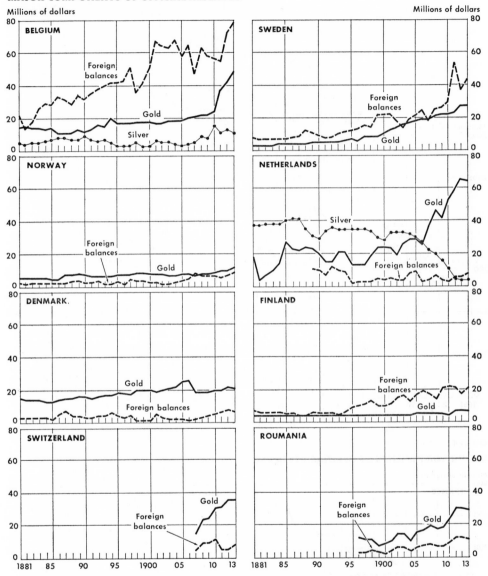

Note: Figures converted into dollars on basis of pre-1914 rates of exchange.

CHART 3

## MAJOR COMPONENTS OF OFFICIAL RESERVES

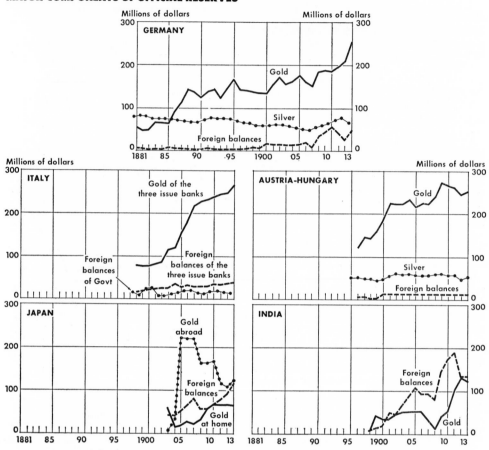

Note: Figures converted into dollars on basis of pre-1914 rates of exchange.

CHART 4

## MAJOR COMPONENTS OF OFFICIAL RESERVES

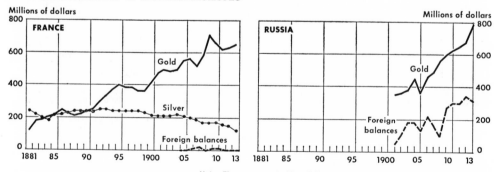

Note: Figures converted into dollars on basis of pre-1914 rates of exchange.

*18*

Sweden. On the other hand, there was no marked consistency over the period with regard to the behavior of the ratio of gold to gold and foreign exchange as among the various countries. The number of cases in which that ratio fell was only somewhat larger than that in which it rose.

The movement of official silver holdings, in those few countries where such holdings are shown in the charts, showed no uniform pattern. In Holland and France the trend was unmistakably downward, due to net exports or drains into internal circulation. On the other hand, the total remained relatively stable in the case of Austria-Hungary and actually rose somewhat in Belgium.

### Official Foreign-Exchange Operations

If we define a gold-exchange standard, according to the present-day usage of that term, as one under which the international monetary reserves of a country with fixed (or periodically adjustable) exchange rates are held not only in gold but also in relatively substantial part in short-term claims on foreigners, then the statistics presented in the preceding sections indicate that the monetary systems of many of the countries there mentioned could be said to have conformed to such a standard during part or all of the period 1880 to 1914. But of more interest, in the context of the pre-1914 gold standard, than official holdings of foreign exchange, as such, was the fact that the authorities concerned resorted to official purchases and sales of foreign exchange against local currency as a supplement to, and in some cases virtual substitute for, the mechanism of private gold arbitraging as a means of keeping exchange rates within limits corresponding to the gold points.[28] This aspect of the pre-1914 gold-exchange-standard arrangements, and the official short-term capital movements which it involved, will be discussed briefly here.[29]

[28] Before 1914 a number of countries, notably Canada, Australia, and New Zealand, had gold-exchange-standard systems that were operated not by the authorities, but by the commercial banks. Since these systems did not involve *official* short-term capital movements, they are excluded from this section and will be touched upon later. See below, pp. 47-48.

[29] In the earlier literature much stress was laid upon the fact that another distinguishing feature of the pre-1914 gold-exchange standard was the absence or limited amount of gold coin in circulation in the countries concerned, whether because the authorities did not *freely* redeem their currencies into gold or because the public preferred other forms of circulating media. See, e.g., J. M. Keynes, *Indian Currency and Finance* (London, 1913); G. Icard, *Un Nouveau Régime Monétaire: Le Gold Exchange Standard* (Montpelier, 1912); and F. Machlup, *Die Goldkernwährung* (Halberstadt, 1925).

Some of the clearest examples of the pre-1914 gold-exchange stand-ard were provided by a number of Asiatic countries whose currencies, long tied to the fluctuating fortunes of silver, were stabilized in terms of gold around the turn of the century. Included in this group were India, the Philippines, Ceylon,[30] Siam,[31] and the Straits Settlements. Some of these countries formally adopted gold-exchange-standard arrangements; others like India drifted into them. While the legal and institutional arrangements differed from country to country—the Indian system being the most complex—the *modus operandi* was essentially the same in all these cases. Briefly, the government or one of its agencies maintained the local currency (mainly silver coin and paper notes) on a par with gold by standing ready to sell and buy foreign exchange at fixed maximum and minimum rates in terms of local currency. For this purpose the authorities kept a stock of foreign exchange (e.g., sterling in the case of India and dollars in the case of the Philippines), and also in some instances gold, at home and abroad. Such gold could always be sold, if need be, to acquire additional foreign exchange to support the exchange rate. For these countries the gold-exchange standard provided the cheapest and most convenient method of keep-ing their currencies on a par with gold and enabled them to do so without permitting free redeemability of their currencies into gold.

In this category of countries, the system maintained by the Philip-pines after 1903 illustrates best the working of this mechanism in its simplest and most automatic form. Under legislation in that year a theoretical gold peso equal to one-half of an American dollar was created, and a Gold Standard Fund was established to be used exclu-sively to maintain the value of the Philippine currency (silver coin and certificates) at this gold parity. Part of the Fund was held in dollar balances in New York and part in local currency in Manila. The Philip-pine Treasurer was directed to sell on demand in Manila drafts on the Fund's balances in New York at a fixed rate in terms of pesos. Con-

[30] As far back as 1884 the Commissioners of Currency in Ceylon had kept the local paper money stable in terms of Indian rupee coin by freely converting the one into the other. After 1903, however, soon after the stabilization of the rupee, they began where possible to issue notes against rupee and sterling exchange, and to sell such exchange against notes, at fixed rates. See Shenoy, *op.cit.*, pp. 91-93, 152-159.

[31] Siam actually went on to the gold-exchange standard late in 1902, but the rates at which the Siamese Treasury stood ready to buy and sell sterling drafts against baht were successively lowered no less than 16 times between 1902 and 1908, when the baht was finally stabilized. See J. C. Ingram, *Economic Change in Siam* (Stanford, 1955), pp. 152-155.

versely, the Philippine depositories in New York stood ready to sell on demand peso drafts on the Fund's balance in Manila at a fixed rate in terms of dollars. There was a small spread between the two rates, corresponding to the theoretical gold points. If the peso fell to the gold export point, pesos would be paid into that part of the Fund held in Manila and dollars out of that part of the Fund held in New York; and conversely if the peso rose to the gold import point. The system, which was purely automatic, enabled the silver peso to be maintained at a parity with the dollar and thus other gold currencies; the Philippine Government made a profit on the spread between the buying and selling rates and earned interest on its reserve in New York; and changes in official dollar balances served as an effective substitute for international gold movements.

Similar systems were set up after 1900 in Panama and a few other Central American countries. A somewhat less rigid form of gold-exchange standard prevailed in Java from as far back as 1875, managed in this case by the central bank rather than a government fund. Among Asiatic countries, Japan is also believed to have operated what was in effect a gold-exchange standard after 1897 when it returned to gold. The Yokohama Specie Bank served as the agency buying and selling foreign exchange against yen on behalf of the government and the Bank of Japan. For this purpose, as already noted, the Japanese authorities held large stocks of foreign exchange and gold under earmark abroad, these stocks being periodically replenished, given the pattern of Japan's balance of payments, by official borrowing operations on overseas markets. Argentina and Brazil were often cited in the earlier literature as examples of the gold-exchange standard from 1900 and from 1906, respectively, but they did not seem to fit the conditions because the government agencies concerned (Conversion Offices) stood ready to buy and sell only *gold* at fixed rates against local currency and did not operate in or hold foreign exchange.

Features of the gold-exchange standard, although more flexible in form, also characterized the monetary systems of many of the European countries whose currencies were tied legally or *de facto* to gold. Since most of these systems were hybrid in character, it is not easy in all cases to label them precisely. But what is relevant here is that the great majority of European central banks, in some cases in conjunction with their governments, from time to time intervened actively in the exchange market to smooth out seasonal and erratic fluctuations in exchange rates and to prevent rates from moving to the gold points (especially the gold export point) at which private arbitrage shipments of gold would have become profitable.[32] Official exchange operations, when undertaken, eliminated the need for to-and-fro gold movements occurring within short periods of time, made possible a more precise influence on exchange rates than exclusive reliance upon the machinery of gold arbitrage, and prevented or kept to a minimum exports of gold that might have a greater adverse psychological effect upon the market than did the equivalent loss of official foreign-exchange reserves involved in supporting the exchange rate. Since, moreover, the authorities usually sold foreign exchange near the gold export point and bought it near the gold import point, these operations yielded a profit over and above the return obtained on the holdings of foreign exchange itself.

Although foreign-exchange policy as an instrument of monetary control was extensively discussed before 1914, concrete information as to the extent of the actual exchange operations of European central banks is extremely limited. Even the official and semi-official histories of the banks concerned, some written in more recent years, throw little light on this matter, valuable though they might be in providing material relating to the background and broad mechanics of these operations.

It is clear that statistics of official *holdings* of foreign exchange and gold, such as were presented in Charts 2, 3, and 4, can give few if any clues as to the relative importance in individual countries of official purchases and sales of foreign exchange, as compared with private gold arbitrage, in maintaining exchange-rate stability within the gold points. For extensive intervention by the authorities in the exchange market need not necessarily have involved relatively large exchange holdings. The authorities could have held the bulk of their reserves in gold but still intervened in the market on a large scale with the aid of a small working balance in foreign exchange. That balance could have been replenished when needed by official gold sales on foreign markets; and any "excess" holdings could have been converted into gold by official purchases abroad. Indeed, there is reason to believe that some of the central banks most active in foreign-exchange operations behaved in precisely that way. By the same token, relatively

[32] While all of the central banks concerned were legally obliged to buy gold at given prices, not all of them were obliged to redeem their currencies freely into gold. In other cases obstacles were placed in the way of commercial banks attempting to obtain gold for export when the gold export point was reached. Sometimes the official selling or buying prices of gold were altered slightly, involving fractional displacements of the gold points.

large official gold holdings could have mainly reflected official purchases abroad rather than purchases from private gold arbitrageurs.

Conversely, large official exchange holdings in relation to gold were not necessarily indicative of an active foreign-exchange policy. A central bank might simply have chosen to convert into foreign exchange, for income-earning purposes, part of its current acquisitions of gold from private importers by the resale of that gold on foreign markets. In the case of Belgium and Sweden, moreover, it will be recalled that official exchange holdings were inflated by the inclusion of exchange held by special government institutions not engaged in exchange-stabilization activities as such.

Only in the case of one European country do the statistics of official exchange and gold holdings themselves point strongly to a heavy reliance by the authorities on exchange operations in maintaining exchange-rate stability: that of Finland. Although that country, after its adoption of the gold standard in 1877, was legally bound to buy and sell gold at fixed prices, exchange rates were kept within the gold points almost exclusively by purchases and sales of foreign exchange by the Bank of Finland. For, as Chart 2 indicates, the Bank's gold holdings remained virtually unchanged continuously from 1880 to 1904, whereas during that same period its exchange holdings underwent considerable fluctuations. During these years, moreover, gold imports and exports (monetary and non-monetary) were nil. These facts point to the conclusion that the Bank of Finland must have kept exchange rates stable by standing ready to buy and sell foreign exchange just within the limits of the gold points. Although in 1905 to 1913 there were monetary gold imports into Finland of some 28 million marks, it is probable that these were on official account and merely represented the conversion into gold of part of the Bank's accumulating exchange holdings rather than private gold-arbitrage shipments.[33]

Austria-Hungary provides the best-known European example of official foreign-exchange operations before 1914.[34] In 1892, after a long period of fluctuating exchange rates, that country took a number of measures looking forward to the adoption of a full gold standard within

[33] During the same period the Bank's gold stock rose by only 14 million marks, suggesting, if the gold-import statistics are correct, that the difference reflected gold that went into circulation or into industry and the arts. Internal gold-coin circulation, however, is known to have been relatively small. A small amount of gold may have been held by the commercial banks.

[34] See, e.g., L. von Mises, "The Foreign Exchange Policy of the Austro-Hungarian Bank," *Economic Journal*, 1909, pp. 201-211.

a few years. These included the creation of a new monetary unit defined in terms of gold, an obligation imposed upon the Austro-Hungarian Bank to buy gold freely at a fixed price, the provision for a gold coinage,[35] and the negotiation of a large gold loan abroad. But no legal obligation was imposed upon the Bank to redeem its currency in gold; and this provision remained suspended throughout the balance of the pre-1914 period. Nevertheless, from 1896 to 1914 the Bank was able to maintain the Austrian crown on a parity with gold as a result of a skillful foreign-exchange policy, aided by a strongly favorable balance of payments.

The Bank would characteristically sell foreign exchange just before the theoretical gold export point was reached and buy exchange just below the gold import point. If it happened to be running short of foreign exchange at any time it would replenish its stock by sales of gold abroad; and any "excess" holdings of foreign exchange would be converted into gold on foreign markets. At times, however, it allowed the exchange rate to reach the gold import point and bought gold freely from private arbitrageurs. Indeed, on occasion it encouraged private gold imports by interest-free advances to gold importers. But gold exports appear to have been undertaken almost exclusively by the authorities themselves. Private parties rarely sought gold for export, even when they could have got it, simply because the Bank seldom permitted exchange rates to rise to the level at which private gold exports would have been profitable. On the other hand, the Bank on occasion allowed the exchange rate to go beyond the theoretical gold point with the deliberate purpose of discouraging outflows of private short-term capital through uncovered interest-arbitrage operations. Austria-Hungary also provides one of the relatively few examples before 1914 of official operations in the *forward* exchange market. These operations, by influencing the forward premium or discount, were designed to discourage outflows, and on at least one occasion unwanted inflows, of private funds through *covered* interest arbitrage.[36]

It is unnecessary here to recite such relatively meager details as are available regarding the nature and extent of official exchange operations in other European countries. The central banks of Belgium, Hol-

---

[35] Actually very little gold coin circulated in Austria-Hungary after 1892 because of the public's preference for silver coins and paper currency. An attempt by the Austro-Hungarian Bank in 1901 to force gold coins into circulation proved a failure, the coin being quickly returned to the Bank.

[36] On the latter point, see P. Einzig, *A Dynamic Theory of Forward Exchange* (London, 1961), pp. 408-409.

sterling and nearly all of the other leading gold currencies was never seriously in question. On the other hand, official balances appear at times to have been shifted from center to center in substantial volume for political or other reasons, with resulting disturbances to the countries from which such balances were withdrawn. Official Russian balances seem to have been the most volatile in this respect. As early as 1894, for example, it was stated that "the [London] market has learnt by experience that the balances of the Russian Government are moved about in a perplexingly capricious way, and are liable to be withdrawn at inopportune times."[40]

Concern was also periodically expressed in some of the countries in which foreign official balances were placed as to the volume of these balances and the possibility of their precipitate withdrawal. Indeed, as far back as 1873, Bagehot had evidenced some anxiety as to the stability of the London money market in view of the possibility of a sudden liquidation of a large German Government balance held in London.[41] There is also some reason to believe that the Bank of England, and doubtless the central banks in some of the other countries in which large amounts of official foreign balances were placed, on occasion took account of these (and private) foreign short-term liabilities, along with other considerations, in framing their credit policies.[42] In general, however, while the possibility of sudden conversions of official balances into gold on a large scale from autonomous causes always existed, the motives for such conversions in the conditions of the pre-1914 gold-standard world were much less compelling than they have been since that time. On the whole, movements of official short-term funds appear to have exerted relatively few disturbing effects of the sort or magnitude that have been witnessed in more recent decades and which are a source of such concern in various quarters today. On the other hand, *private* short-term capital flows, as will be noted below, may at times have been somewhat more disturbing in their effects.

[40] *Economist*, November 17, 1894, p. 1399. According to the *Bankers Magazine*, June 1891, p. 977, when Barings' credit began to shake in the summer of 1890, the Russian Government withdrew balances in London and almost precipitated a crisis.

[41] W. Bagehot, *Lombard Street* (London, 1912 edition), pp. 310-320.

[42] Sayers states that this was so in the case of the Bank of England. R. S. Sayers, *Bank of England Operations, 1890-1914* (London, 1936), p. 118. The *Economist* (June 10, 1899, p. 826), spoke of the need for the Bank of England to hold larger reserves against the deposits of foreign governments likely to be drawn upon heavily from time to time than against ordinary bank deposits.

which the Bank was subject. Nevertheless, at no time during the period was the continued convertibility of sterling seriously questioned or convertibility itself seriously threatened. The Bank of England chose to minimize its holdings of non-income-earning gold and to rely instead upon its ability in case of need to influence the flow of private short-term capital in an equilibrating direction by use of discount-rate policy and related techniques.

In certain other gold-standard countries, including Germany, concern was also expressed about the adequacy of official reserves, especially in the later years of the period, and special efforts were made to economize further on the use of gold at home. Several countries, when confronted with serious pressures on their reserves, were forced to take "extraordinary" measures to protect convertibility, including special borrowings from abroad, liberalization of central-bank reserve requirements, and in two cases temporary application of a limited form of exchange control.[43] But no leading country was ever forced to abandon gold or to devalue its currency. In general, there was widespread confidence in the ability of the authorities to maintain existing gold parities. Under these conditions, private short-term capital movements proved for the most part an important source of support to official reserves at times of strain.[44]

Recent discussions have made it clear that there is no really satisfactory way of measuring the "adequacy" of a country's international monetary reserves or indeed of precisely defining the concept itself. Even on the assumption that before 1914 the primary purpose of reserves was to finance temporary payments deficits and to maintain confidence in the exchange stability of gold currencies, one cannot specify in quantitative terms what constituted an "adequate" level of reserves for a given country at a given time. That would have depended, among many other things, upon that country's degree of susceptibility to large adverse swings in its balances of payments, the kind of financial policies it pursued, the degree of public confidence in its ability and willingness to follow appropriate policies, its ability in case of need to borrow abroad and to attract inflows of private short-term funds, and the extent to which its reserves were "locked up" in legal reserve requirements behind central-bank liabilities. By the same token, there is no really satisfactory way of measuring trends in the adequacy of a country's reserves over time, or of comparing the adequacy of the reserves of different countries at a given point of time.

[43] See my *Monetary Policy*, pp. 56-59, and below, pp. 84-85.
[44] See below, pp. 43-44.

A very crude and imperfect approximation to measuring *changes* in the degree of adequacy of a country's reserves over time—which leaves aside the question of the appropriateness of reserves on the base date— would be to trace the behavior of the ratio of that country's reserves to its imports. A fall in that ratio might be considered a rough indication of a deterioration in the degree of adequacy of reserves, and a rise of an improvement. But it is clear that the volume of imports is only one factor influencing a country's need for reserves, although admittedly an important one, and that there is no reason to believe that the need for reserves should grow proportionately with imports. Nevertheless, in the absence of any more satisfactory measure, and because so much use has been made of such ratios for the post-1914 period by respected authorities,[45] calculations of annual ratios of reserves to imports have been made for 10 selected gold-standard countries for the period 1880-1913. They are presented here for whatever little value or historical interest they might have.[46]

The results, shown in Charts 5 and 6, reveal a variety of patterns. The trend in the ratios for the United States, France, and Sweden was sharply upward, indeed so much so for the first two of these countries as to suggest strongly that the degree of adequacy of their reserves improved markedly over a period as a whole, regardless of other factors besides imports that might have been at work increasing their need for reserves. On the other hand, the ratios for Denmark, Norway, and Finland, while fluctuating sharply from year to year, showed a downward trend, which might or might not have indicated a deterioration in the degree of reserve adequacy for these countries. Finally, in the case of England, Holland, Germany, and Belgium, the ratios showed no marked trend in one direction or the other over the period. Here, too, it would be illegitimate to draw any firm conclusions as to the trend of reserve adequacy.

[45] E.g., International Monetary Fund, *International Reserves and Liquidity* (Washington, 1958); and R. Triffin, *Gold and the Dollar Crisis* (New Haven, 1961).

[46] In most cases the ratios were computed from year-end official holdings of gold and foreign exchange (gold alone for the United States and Great Britain) and the annual value of imports for that year. For France, Germany, and Great Britain, annual averages of monthly official reserve holdings were used. The data for official gold and foreign-exchange reserves are the same as those used in Charts 2, 3, and 4; for the United States and Great Britain we used the gold stock of the U.S. Treasury and the Bank of England. The merchandise import figures for the various countries were taken from statistical yearbooks or other official sources. Although official holdings of silver have been excluded from monetary reserves, they might have properly been included in a few cases.

It would be even more dangerous to use the various ratios for purposes of inter-country comparisons of relative reserve adequacy. The
factors determining the need for reserves undoubtedly differed widely
from country to country. Nevertheless, the wide differences among the
average ratios for most of the countries over the period as a whole is
striking. Most marked were the differences in the average levels of the
ratios for the United States and France,[47] on the one hand, and for

CHART 5

**GROSS OFFICIAL RESERVES (GOLD AND FOREIGN EXCHANGE)
AS A PERCENTAGE OF IMPORTS**

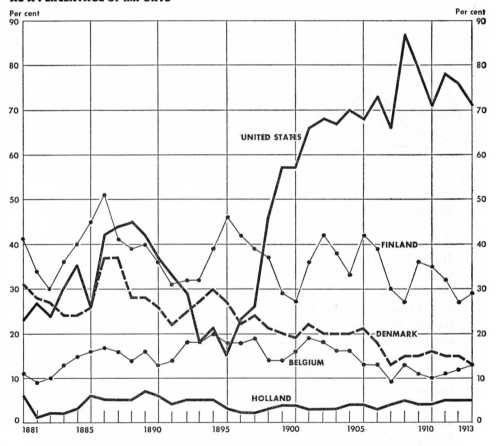

[47] Worthy of note also is the fact that the ratio for Russia, not shown in the
charts, remained consistently above 100 per cent from 1901 to 1913, and almost hit
200 per cent in 1909. The Japanese ratio, also not shown, was in the neighborhood
of 100 per cent for many of the years after 1900.

31

CHART 6

**GROSS OFFICIAL RESERVES (GOLD AND FOREIGN EXCHANGE)
AS A PERCENTAGE OF IMPORTS**

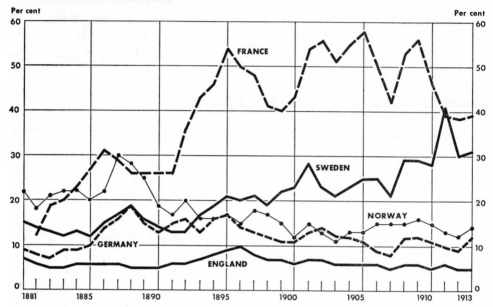

England and Holland, on the other. So marked were these differences that one can safely say that reserves were much more "adequate" for the former than for the latter pair of countries. Yet England and Holland, despite ratios averaging only about 5 per cent over the period, were equally successful in maintaining the gold standard. An attempt to explain the wide differences among ratios from country to country would take us far afield. However, of relevance, among many other factors, were differing minimum legal-reserve requirements among central banks or governments, differing attitudes as to the amount of "excess" reserves they should hold, differing proportions of bank deposits to total money supply, and differing ratios of imports to national income.

Pre-1914 ratios of reserves to imports for the various individual gold-standard countries were generally much lower than the ratios which have prevailed since that time. This does not of course mean that reserves were then less "adequate." In those days, for example, countries could count to a greater extent upon equilibrating movements of private short-term capital; national economies were in better balance with each other; and monetary authorities were more responsive to the discipline of the balance of payments.

A notable feature of international monetary arrangements before 1914 was the virtual absence of any systematic cooperation among monetary authorities. Direct contacts among central banks, except in connection with routine banking operations, were very limited. To be sure, central banks occasionally extended credits or gold loans to one another in time of stress or gave assistance in other ways,[48] but such action was exceptional and was invariably motivated by considerations of narrow self-interest. Central bankers showed little or no overt awareness of their mutual responsibility for the smooth functioning of the international gold standard or of the need for a collaboration based upon mutual interest. In the later years of the period, however, the growing international competition for gold by leading monetary authorities, the disturbing effects of which were most dramatically illustrated during the crisis of 1907, made more evident the need for closer and systematic cooperation. In 1908 the Italian Minister of Finance, Luzzati, recommended a plan for organized inter-central-bank aid and cooperation in the form of gold loans at times of crisis, provision of mutual gold-earmarking facilities, and improved international clearing arrangements.[49] Similar proposals or alternative schemes of cooperation were advanced by others.[50] The International Conference at Brussels in 1912 passed a resolution to the effect that European central banks should hold meetings for the purpose of improving the system of international payments. But these and other recommendations for closer central-bank cooperation and contact met with little response from the authorities concerned.

[48] See Bloomfield, *Monetary Policy*, pp. 56-57. For an example of *regional* central-bank cooperation, see the earlier discussion of the Scandinavian Monetary Union.

[49] L. Luzzati, "Une Conférence Internationale pour la Paix Monétaire," *Séances et Travaux de l'Académie des Sciences Morales et Politiques*, 1908 (I), pp. 358-368.

[50] See, e.g., M. Ansiaux, "La Solidarité Monétaire Internationale," *Revue Economique Internationale*, October 1910, pp. 7-38.

## III. PRIVATE SHORT-TERM CAPITAL MOVEMENTS

It is widely accepted that private short-term capital movements—the other and more interesting component of the international flow of short-term capital—played an important role in the successful functioning of the pre-1914 gold standard. Apart from financing world trade, these movements helped to fill gaps in the balance of payments of a seasonal and short-run character or pending any longer-run adjustments via income and price effects that might be necessary in the event of more persisting payments disequilibrium. Sensitive to interest-rate differentials and to changes in exchange rates within the gold points, these movements are believed to have performed a characteristically equilibrating function in the balance of payments, by reducing the need for movements of official reserves, and to have promoted international financial stability and the integration of national money markets. While this picture is broadly accurate, the nature and role of private short-term capital movements before 1914 have usually been oversimplified and their degree of sensitivity to interest rates and exchange rates exaggerated. At the same time these movements have been endowed with a benign character that they did not always possess.

We may begin with an outline of the kinds, motivations, and general characteristics of these movements during the pre-1914 gold-standard period, with some indication as to the relative importance and geographical orientation of the various components. Attention will be focused mainly on movements between gold-standard countries.

### Kinds and Motivations

Of the aggregate volume of private international short-term claims outstanding at any time, a very substantial part undoubtedly consisted of claims on trade account. Changes in the volume of these claims, resulting from shifts in the volume and pattern of trade that was being financed, involved movements of private short-term capital. With the growth of world trade over the period, the outstanding volume of international commercial debt undoubtedly grew. It has been estimated that by 1913 the amount of such indebtedness totaled about 15 billion Swiss francs ($2.9 billion).[1]

The most direct form of trade credit was the grant of open-book

[1] See Conolly, "Memorandum on the International Short-term Indebtedness," op.cit., p. 363.

34

credits by exporters to importers. More formal was the use of the trade bill drawn directly by exporters on importers and accepted by the latter upon presentation. In other cases the importer would finance his purchases by borrowing directly from a foreign bank. In all these cases a private short-term claim on foreigners (and a corresponding liability) was created.

While all these methods were used before 1914 in financing world trade, of far greater importance was the use of the bank acceptance, especially in the form of sterling bills. London, because of its unrivalled credit facilities and the international standing of sterling, financed not only the great bulk of Britain's own foreign trade but also a very large part of the trade between foreign countries themselves. Exporters, whether foreign or British, would draw bills against their shipments on London accepting houses, or on the branches of foreign and colonial banks in London,[2] which had agreed on behalf of the importers to accept such bills on presentation. By discounting these acceptances with their own local banks, exporters were able to get paid at once,[3] while importers did not have to pay until the maturity of the bills (usually 60 to 90 days), by which time they, or their local banks under whose guarantee the acceptance credits had been arranged, were committed to put the accepting houses in funds. The local banks that discounted the bills for their customers would either hold them until maturity or rediscount them in the London market. The London accepting houses, by substituting their names for those of the importers, were paid a commission without having to use any of their own funds, and they acquired a claim (and assumed a liability) that was in most cases secured by documents evidencing ownership of the goods in shipment or in warehouses. Finally, the sterling bank acceptance provided an admirable money-market instrument for London discount houses and banks and for other institutions or parties, British or foreign, wishing to invest their funds at short term in a liquid sterling asset.

Acceptance financing of foreign trade through London did not of course in all cases bring into existence *international* short-term claims and thereby involve short-term capital movements. That depended upon the nature of the trade transaction that was being financed.

International short-term claims were created in the case of accept-

[2] The London joint-stock banks did not participate actively in the acceptance business until the years just before 1914.

[3] In some cases the exporters would hold the bills until maturity, using their banks as agents to collect the proceeds at maturity.

ance financing of British exports. Here the London accepting houses would acquire claims on the foreign importers or on their local banks which arranged the credits for them. The actual granters of the credits—who would have a corresponding claim on the accepting houses—would be those who bought the bills so created, or the British exporters if they did not choose to discount them. To the extent that the bills happened to be purchased in the London market by foreigners,[4] England's acceptance claims on foreigners would be offset by a foreign short-term liability. Otherwise, the foreign claims in question would have as their counterpart a purely domestic liability.

When British *imports* were financed by acceptance credits through London, the accepting houses would acquire a purely domestic claim on the British importer or his bank. The actual financing of the imports would in effect be provided by those who purchased the foreign-drawn sterling bills in the London market, or by the foreign exporters or their banks if they held the bills until maturity. To the extent that the bills were held by foreigners until maturity or purchased by foreigners in the London market, England's domestic claims would be offset by foreign short-term liabilities. Finally, London acceptance financing of direct trade between foreign countries would result in British short-term claims on foreign importers or their banks. Only if the foreign exporters or their banks held the bills until maturity, or if the foreign-drawn bills on London houses were purchased by foreigners in the London market, would the British claims on foreigners be counterbalanced by short-term foreign liabilities.

It has been assumed above that the financing of trade through the sterling bill, and the short-term capital flows to which it gave rise, were single, isolated transactions. Actually, at any moment of time some of London's outstanding foreign claims on acceptance account[5] were always maturing and some new claims were always being created. Should the two not exactly balance, the outstanding total would rise or fall, involving net outflows or inflows of short-term capital respectively. Such changes could be brought about by shifts in the volume or pattern of trade being financed through London or in the average maturity of the bills, or by other factors. These in turn could be influenced by monetary policy in England or abroad. In the short run, then, the net

[4] Such purchases would not of course be directly related to the trade financing itself and really fall into a different category of short-term capital movements to be discussed below.

[5] Including acceptances not only of commercial bills, but also of finance bills to be discussed below.

movement of funds directly associated with changes in London's outstanding acceptance claims on foreigners could, and most probably did, fluctuate substantially.

Acceptance financing of foreign trade by other countries before 1914 never reached the scale that it did in England, although the purely domestic acceptance was well known and extensively used on the continent. Only in the case of Germany was an aggressive effort made to capture a greater share of the international acceptance business. Although a considerable measure of success appears to have been achieved in the years just before World War I[6] the mark acceptance never attained the status of the sterling bill as an instrument of international trade financing. Of even less importance in this connection was the franc acceptance, which appears to have been used mainly to finance trade between France and its colonies.[7] In Holland, which in the 17th and part of the 18th century had financed a large proportion of world trade, the international acceptance business had long since shrunk to very modest dimensions and in the years just before 1914 was practically limited to the tobacco trade.[8]

Neither the bank acceptance nor the trade acceptance had any important place in the United States before 1914, even with respect to the financing of purely domestic trade. The National Banks were not specifically authorized to accept time bills drawn on them, and other American banks created relatively few acceptances because of the lack of a discount market for them.[9] United States foreign trade was financed predominantly by means of sterling bills drawn on London. The fact that the United States had to pay large sums in commissions each year to London bankers for these services, and that there were other disadvantages resulting from the absence of a dollar acceptance market, was a source of growing discussion and dissatisfaction in this country in the years just before World War I.[10]

[6] J. Reisser, *The German Great Banks and Their Concentration*, National Monetary Commission (Washington, 1911), pp. 431-432; and P. B. Whale, *Joint Stock Banking in Germany* (London, 1930), pp. 89-90.

[7] J. S. G. Wilson, *French Banking Structure and Credit Policy* (London, 1957), p. 156; and P. Coste, *Les Grands Marchés Financiers* (Paris, 1932), p. 20.

[8] G. Vissering and J. W. Holstijn, "The Effect of the War Upon Banking and Currency," in *The Netherlands and the World War* (New Haven, 1928), pp. 82-83. The authors point out at the end of 1913 Dutch acceptances for foreign account amounted to only 25 million guilders ($10 million).

[9] See, e.g., M. G. Myers, *The New York Money Market* (New York, 1931), pp. 315ff.; and W. Ward, *American Commercial Credits* (New York, 1922), pp. 14-15.

[10] See, e.g., L. M. Jacobs, *Bank Acceptances*, National Monetary Commission

In addition to its use in the financing of world trade, the bank acceptance was also employed extensively before 1914, in the form of so-called finance bills, as a means of international short-term borrowing for purposes not directly related to foreign trade. If short-term interest rates were lower in a foreign acceptance center than at home, it would be to the advantage of banks and others in need of short-term funds to arrange to draw finance bills on foreign accepting houses, to discount the accepted bills in the foreign center, and to convert the proceeds into home currency through the foreign-exchange market. In this way needed short-term funds could be acquired more cheaply by borrowing abroad than at home.[11] Indeed, at times the funds might not have been obtainable at home at all. Finance bills were drawn against the deposit of securities or other collateral or against the general credit of the borrower; and the drawers (or the parties that arranged the credits) were of course committed to put the foreign accepting houses in funds before the maturity of the bills.

In assessing the advantages of short-term borrowing abroad instead of at home—assuming that the latter alternative were available—the borrowers would of course also have to consider the possibility of exchange losses that could wipe out or more than offset the gain in interest rates. With regard to gold-standard countries, there was in general widespread confidence in established exchange-rate parities. The extent of the possible exchange loss on borrowing transactions between such countries, being set up by the difference between the prevailing exchange rate and the lower gold point of the borrowing country, was thus approximately known in advance and could be included in the calculation.[12] In fact, if the exchange rate were already at its lower gold point, the possibility of exchange *profits* would give an added stimulus to borrowing and in some cases become its primary rationale.[13] For the

(Washington, 1911), pp. 1-17; and P. M. Warburg, *The Discount System in Europe*, National Monetary Commission (Washington, 1910), pp. 39-43.

[11] The cost of borrowing abroad would include not only the interest rate at which the bills could be discounted in the foreign center, but also the acceptance commission.

[12] Where a country off gold was involved, the borrower would instead usually cover the exchange risk in the forward-exchange market. Such markets existed wherever currencies were not tied to gold or for gold currencies subject to some element of doubt. In such cases the borrowers would have to include in their calculations, along with the difference in interest rates, the cost of forward cover (which could of course in some instances be negative).

[13] Even if the borrowing costs were higher abroad than at home, it might still have paid to borrow abroad if the expected favorable turn in the exchange rate exceeded the extra interest cost.

exchange rate could in general go no lower, and might instead rise above that point by the time the borrowing had to be repaid. A good example is provided by American experience. Before 1914 the dollar tended to be seasonally weak on the exchange market in the spring and early summer, but to strengthen in the late summer and early fall under the impact of large crop shipments abroad. American bankers would borrow in Europe on finance bills in the earlier months in anticipation of repaying these debts later in the year at a profit.[14] Such operations tended to reduce the need for to-and-fro seasonal gold movements and the extent of seasonal variation in the dollar exchange rate.

In actual practice, of course, the gold points were not rigidly fixed even in the short run.[15] Apart from the slight changes that might occur in the costs of shipping gold, some of the leading central banks from time to time fractionally altered their selling or buying prices of gold or took other steps that had the effect of slightly displacing the gold points or of causing exchange rates to move somewhat outside the range of those points.[16] Thus a precise estimate of the possible extent of exchange losses, even when there was perfect confidence in the parities of the currencies concerned, could rarely be made. In general, however, the range of possible variations in exchange rates between nearly all gold currencies could be approximately gauged at any time. On the other hand, whenever the parities of currencies tied to gold (legally or *de facto*) were subject to some measure of doubt, international short-term borrowing or other exchange operations involving such currencies tended to be covered in the forward market. In such cases the relevant comparisons would be between interest-rate differentials and forward discounts or premiums; and indeed it might often have been *profitable* to cover the exchange risk. Einzig has argued that where the Russian ruble and Austrian crown were involved, even

[14] E. W. Kemmerer, *Seasonal Variations in the Relative Demand for Money and Capital in the United States*, National Monetary Commission (Washington, 1910), pp. 140-141.

[15] Nor were they necessarily identical at any time for all gold arbitrageurs or for all kinds of gold shipments.

[16] Morgenstern's failure to take account of these considerations was one of the reasons for his underestimation of the actual range of the gold points in the pre-1914 period and the extent to which those points were subject to fluctuation. It led him to the conclusion, on the basis of his detailed statistical investigation, that the gold points for the dollar, franc, pound, and mark were frequently "violated" by exchange rates, i.e., to the conclusion that the exchange rates between pairs of these currencies were often and persistently beyond (what he regarded as) the gold points. See *International Financial Transactions*, pp. 169-211, 241-276.

after their stabilization in terms of gold, such operations were almost always covered. Unfortunately, we have far too little concrete information on the extent of covered operations between gold-standard countries before 1914 or on the activity of forward-exchange markets therein. The research of Einzig,[17] who almost alone has investigated this area, would suggest that forward-exchange operations between such countries were more common than has been believed.

The initiative in finance-bill operations—to resume the discussion—did not always have to come from the *borrower*. If short-term interest-rate differentials and exchange rates were such as to make short-term capital exports from a given country advantageous, banks in that country, as one means of effecting such exports, could ask their foreign correspondents to draw bills on them for acceptance and to invest on their behalf the proceeds of such bills, when discounted in the accepting center, in the foreign money market concerned. Or a bank could draw a finance bill on one center in order to use the proceeds not at home but for short-term investment in a third country.

Short-term borrowing abroad on finance bills was widely resorted to before 1914. The bulk of such drawings was made on London,[18] but Paris[19] and certain other continental centers[20] were at times substantial lenders in this way. The largest short-term borrowers through this medium were the United States, Germany, and Russia. American finance bills, for example, grew rapidly in importance after 1900 and, in addition to the seasonal drawings noted above, became an important instrument for bolstering the resources of the New York money market during periods of rising interest rates and growing stock-market specu-

[17] P. Einzig, *The Theory of Forward Exchange* (London, 1937), pp. 31-60. The process of covering before 1914 often involved buying or selling of long foreign-currency bills, necessitating immediate cash outlays, rather than purchases or sales of forward exchange in the modern sense.

[18] It has been estimated that of the £350 million ($1,715 million) of prime bank acceptances outstanding in the London market in 1913, some 60 per cent consisted of finance bills. See the remarks of Sir Robert Kindersley, *Minutes of Evidence before the Committee on Finance and Industry* (London, 1931), Vol. I, p. 76.

[19] E. Kaufmann, *La Banque en France* (Paris, 1914), p. 300. One writer has pointed out, however, that the total amount of acceptance credits granted to foreigners by French banks was much smaller before 1914 than their short-term foreign credits granted in other forms. See L. Pommery, "Le Marché de Paris et les Acceptations de Banque," *Revue d'Economie Politique*, March-April 1929, p. 288.

[20] In addition to Berlin, some finance bills were drawn by foreigners on smaller acceptance centers, such as Amsterdam. See A. Houwink, *Acceptcrediet* (Amsterdam, 1929), p. 30.

lation. At the beginning of 1903 the outstanding amount of American finance bills, held mainly in England and France, was estimated to have amounted to between $300-500 million,[21] and during the stock-market boom of 1906 the total was placed at $400-500 million.[22] In that year, and on other occasions during the early 1900's, the total was regarded as so large that the Bank of England and several other European central banks discriminated against American finance bills in an effort to check the outflow of capital associated with these borrowings.

An important form of international short-term borrowing, motivated by essentially the same considerations as the drawing of finance bills, was the system, especially popular on the continent, of so-called bill pensioning. While taking a number of variations, this system consisted essentially of an arrangement whereby the borrowing banks would obtain short-term funds from abroad by discounting domestic bills in their portfolios with foreign banks under repurchase agreements whereby the bills would be bought back by the time of their maturity on the basis of the same rate of exchange at which the pensions had originally been arranged. The lenders, although purchasing an asset denominated in the borrower's currency, were thus protected against any exchange risk. As in the case of borrowing by means of finance bills, bill pensioning abroad would be advantageous to the borrower if the discount rate in the foreign center was lower than the rate at which the bills could be discounted at home, after allowance for the exchange risk that the borrower might be assuming or in some cases for the cost of covering that risk in the forward market. Not only banks but also business firms at times borrowed abroad in this way, usually under the guarantee of their local banks.

The largest borrowers *en pension* before 1914 were Germany and Russia,[23] with French banks providing most of the funds in question. German bills pensioned in Paris are estimated to have at times reached outstanding totals of as much as 1 billion marks (about $240 million), a huge sum for those days.[24] French banks are reported to have given

[21] A. Margraff, *International Exchange* (Chicago, 1904), pp. 34-35.

[22] O. M. W. Sprague, *History of Crises Under the National Banking System*, National Monetary Commission (Washington, 1910), p. 230; and A. D. Noyes, *Forty Years of American Finance* (New York, 1909), p. 355.

[23] For Germany, see Reisser, *The German Great Banks*, pp. 212-214; and W. Prion, *Das deutsche Wechseldiskontgeschäft* (Leipzig, 1907), pp. 202-204. For Russia, see E. Epstein, *Les Banques de Commerce Russes* (Paris, 1925), pp. 41-42; and J. Lewin, *Der Heutige Zustand der Aktienhandelsbanken in Russland, 1900-1910* (Freiburg, 1912), p. 38.

[24] M. Palyi, "The Meaning of the Gold Standard," *Journal of Business of the*

credits in this form, not only to Germany and Russia, but also to Austria-Hungary, the Scandinavian countries, Italy, Belgium, Switzerland, and even the United States and England.[25] The Russian State Bank between 1900 and 1909 actually encouraged bill pensioning and related short-term borrowings abroad by Russian banks and enterprises by providing them through swap transactions with forward-exchange cover at minimal cost.[26]

Influenced by similar factors as international short-term borrowing via finance bills, bill pensioning, and related techniques, and in many instances almost indistinguishable from it, were interest-arbitrage operations. These operations, which were undertaken mainly at the initiative of lenders as contrasted with borrowers, involved the transfer of liquid funds from one country to another in order to profit from differences in yields on short-term investments after allowance for the possibility of exchange losses (uncovered arbitrage) or for the cost of covering the risk in the forward market (covered arbitrage). So far as concerned interest arbitrage between countries firmly on a gold basis, the exchange risk as a general rule was not covered because of confidence that the exchange rate would move only within narrow limits approximating the gold points, although those points as noted earlier were subject to the possibility of slight displacements. It has been said, at least so far as Great Britain was involved, that uncovered interest arbitrage was the "classic kind" of movement of short-term funds

---

University of Chicago, July 1944, p. 298. In Roumania, for which an exact figure is available, the nine main commercial banks had outstanding in 1913 a total of 330 million lei (about $16 million) of borrowings en pension from abroad, mainly from Germany and Austria. See E. Ené, Les Banques en Roumanie (Paris, 1915), pp. 84-85.

[25] Kaufmann, La Banque en France, pp. 264-265.

[26] In view of the element of doubt as to the exchange stability of the ruble after its attachment to gold, Russian short-term borrowings from abroad were almost invariably covered against the exchange risk. Although short-term interest rates were generally lower in other European centers than in Russia, the discount on the forward ruble at certain seasons of the year often rose to a point at which short-term borrowings from abroad became unattractive, and Russian banks would turn instead to the State Bank. In order to encourage borrowings from abroad, the State Bank in 1900 agreed, for a small commission, to sell foreign exchange to the borrowers, when their debts fell due, at the same rate against rubles as that at which the Bank had originally bought the foreign exchange from them. In effect, the Bank provided low-cost forward cover, thereby enabling Russian banks and firms to take advantage of the lower interest rates abroad. In February 1904 the Bank's forward commitments under this scheme reached a peak of 271 million rubles ($141 million). See Slansky, La Banque Impériale de Russie, pp. 93-94; and Epstein, Les Banques de Commerce Russes, pp. 41-42.

under the pre-1914 gold standard;[27] and that the short-run effectiveness of a rise in the Bank of England discount rate depended in substantial part upon the fact that funds moved to London *without* the exchange risk being covered.[28] With regard to transactions between some of the other gold-standard countries, however, covered interest arbitrage might, as suggested earlier, have been more common than is usually believed.

Interest arbitrage could take place not only between the arbitrageur's home country and a foreign center, but could also be effected by the arbitrageur between two foreign countries. In some cases it might have been combined with a borrowing operation, the arbitrageur borrowing funds at home or abroad for investment in a third country. Here the relevant interest-rate comparison would have been between the borrowing rate and the rate at which the funds could be invested. The relative availability of funds in the country in which funds were to be borrowed would also have to be considered along with interest rates. Moreover, even if the comparison were one between yields on short-term *investments* in two centers, those yields need not have related to *identical* kinds of investments. In general, the rate on bank acceptances (bill rate) was the relevant basis for comparison in interest arbitrage between the leading money markets, although rates on Treasury bills, call loans, and even time deposits sometimes played a part. With regard to transactions involving the United States, where no market for bank acceptances existed, the relevant rates were those on commercial paper and call loans. In those countries where no money markets existed, even if they were on the gold standard, foreign interest-arbitrage funds could hardly have been expected to be attracted at all, except perhaps into time deposits.

There has been general agreement that under the pre-1914 gold standard private short-term capital movements played primarily a short-run equilibrating role in the balance of payments by tending to reduce the size of gold flows or changes in official exchange holdings, i.e., by tending to offset other balance-of-payments items causing move-

[27] Evidence submitted by the Bank of England in *Principal Memoranda of Evidence Submitted to the Committee on the Working of the Monetary System* [Radcliffe Committee], Vol. I (London, 1960), p. 42.

[28] C. P. Kindleberger, *International Economics*, revised edition (Homewood, Illinois, 1958), p. 333. As Kindleberger points out, if no one was prepared to take a long position in sterling, a rise in short-run interest rates in London would simply have tended to bring about an offsetting change in the forward sterling rate so as to eliminate any incentive for transferring liquid funds to London.

ments of official reserves.[29] A decline in the exchange rate of a currency to its gold export point would tend to encourage stabilizing speculation in that currency in view of the belief that it could not fall (much) farther and might instead subsequently recover. Short-term interest-rate differentials, which would also be included in the calculation as to the profitability of moving funds, would often *reinforce* the effect of the exchange-rate movement in view of a tendency for short-term interest rates to be relatively high in the country losing reserves, whether because of discount-rate increases or not. Conversely, when a country's currency was at or near its gold import point and the authorities were gaining reserves, the belief that the exchange rate could not rise (much) farther and might instead subsequently decline would be an inducement to short-term capital outflows which would often be strengthened by a tendency for short-term interest rates to be relatively low at such time in the country concerned. To the extent that this short-run equilibrating mechanism functioned, it was dependent, as we have seen, upon implicit confidence in the exchange-rate parities of the currencies involved and upon a conviction that exchange rates would move only within narrow limits approximating existing gold points.

Even within such a framework, however, short-term capital flows between gold-standard countries were by no means always equilibrating in character. Often they caused or accentuated movements of official reserves rather than substituted for them. For example, the stimulus to short-term capital inflows caused by a fall in a country's exchange rate to its gold export point could have been more than offset by higher interest rates abroad than at home, thereby resulting in outflows rather than inflows of capital and in increased rather than decreased exports of gold. Or a sudden rise in short-term interest rates in an important financial center, whether associated with a payments deficit or not, could attract short-term funds from other countries that had been in a balanced payments position or already in deficit, thus causing or increasing reserve drains from the latter. Such outflows of funds would be disequilibrating from the viewpoint of these particular countries, even if they happened to be equilibrating from the viewpoint of the country which had attracted them. Again, movements of short-term funds might at times have occurred in response to interest-

[29] See the explicit statements of J. Viner, *Studies in the Theory of International Trade* (New York, 1937), pp. 403-404; Kindleberger, *International Economics*, p. 325; and R. Nurkse, *International Currency Experience* (Princeton, 1944), pp. 14-15.

and exchange-rate incentives on a scale which *more* than offset ("overcompensated") a payments deficit or surplus, thereby causing an actual *reversal* in the movement of official reserves and to that extent being disequilibrating in character. Moreover, not all categories of short-term capital flows were directly related to interest rates or exchange rates at all, and there is no reason why they should have necessarily been equilibrating from the viewpoint of the countries from which or to which the capital moved or both. But the important thing to note is that all such disequilibrating movements of short-term funds probably could not have persisted for long on any sizeable scale, at least for the countries losing reserves, for such countries usually reacted to continuing reserve drains by raising their discount rates or taking other defensive measures, the effectiveness of which admittedly varied much from country to country.

The equilibrating role of private short-term capital movements was always subject to the limitation that such funds were not perfectly mobile internationally.[30] At any time the amount that could or would move abroad in response to short-term interest-rate differentials and movements in the exchange rate was by no means unlimited. This consideration no doubt accounts in some part for the "comparatively large permanent differences" in pre-1914 short-term interest rates among the four leading gold-standard countries which Morgenstern found rather remarkable.[31] It may also help to explain his findings that the Goschen-Weill solidarity hypothesis, which he subjected to a detailed statistical investigation, was frequently violated.[32]

In addition to the international short-term borrowing and lending operations discussed above, a number of other kinds of private short-term capital movements before 1914 merit brief consideration.

Various governments, including their subdivisions such as munici-

[30] See, e.g., Viner, *Studies*, pp. 405-406; and R. G. Hawtrey, "The Gold Standard and the Balance of Payments," *Economic Journal*, March 1926, pp. 65-66.

[31] Morgenstern, *International Financial Transactions*, pp. 160-163.

[32] *Ibid.*, pp. 166-168, 302ff. The solidarity hypotheses, briefly stated, is that short-term interest-rate differentials between two gold currencies cannot normally exceed the maximum extent of the possible exchange risk due to a movement of the exchange rate to the gold point. Another reason for the observed violations would seem to lie in Morgenstern's statistical treatment of the gold points referred to briefly above. He also worked on the assumption that international movements of short-term funds among the four gold-standard countries were never covered against the exchange risk. To the extent that there was such covering, we would have another possible reason for the observed violations. See the penetrating review of Morgenstern's book by G. H. Borts in *Journal of the American Statistical Association*, March 1960, pp. 223-228.

palities, as well as large business firms, at times borrowed abroad in large volume by placing their own *short-term* obligations on foreign markets, often in anticipation of flotations of long-term issues that had to be postponed because of unreceptive market conditions. It has been stated, for example, that foreign Treasury bills were "regularly placed" in the London market when the City was temporarily unwilling to absorb long-term loans on terms acceptable to the foreign borrowers concerned; these bills were later redeemed out of the proceeds of long-term issues.[33] In the last few years of the period, moreover, the financing of wars and armaments by sales of Treasury bills and short-term notes on foreign markets, including London, became increasingly common.[34] Early in 1913 it was noted that "London is still stuffed full of short-term notes and short-dated securities issued by hard-up governments and extravagant [foreign] corporations."[35] Paris was also reported at that time to have held large quantities of such notes.[36]

Commercial banks had at all times to keep minimum deposit balances in one or more foreign financial centers in order to meet the daily demands of their customers for foreign exchange, to keep their deposit accounts abroad alive, and to meet any requirements for "compensating" balances against credits extended to them by foreign banks and accepting houses. The outstanding volume of such balances would tend to fluctuate from day to day in an accommodating fashion depending upon the demand for and supply of foreign exchange. Should these balances tend to fall below working needs, the banks would quickly replenish them; and any balances in excess of minimum requirements would be invested at short-term in foreign money markets or repatriated, depending upon interest rates, exchange rates, or related considerations. It is likely that some large business firms with overseas connections may have also maintained working balances in those foreign countries with which they had close business dealings, although such balances may have often been held through the intermediary of the firms' local banks.

Some private short-term capital movements were always taking place as a result of *long-term* foreign borrowings. On the one hand, the proceeds of private long-term borrowings on foreign capital markets were

---

[33] W. A. Brown, Jr., *The International Gold Standard Reinterpreted, 1914-1934* (New York, 1940), Vol. I, pp. 661-662.

[34] *Economist*, December 14, 1912, pp. 1205-1206.

[35] *Ibid.*, April 15, 1913, pp. 805-806. Many of the corporations involved were said to be American.

[36] *Ibid.*, July 26, 1913, p. 159.

not usually drawn down all at once, but were left in the lending centers to be utilized as needed. In effect, the long-term capital outflows from the lending countries were offset in part by accommodating private short-term capital inflows. On the other hand, it was the usual custom for the borrowers to accumulate balances in the lending countries some weeks ahead of pending payments for interest and principal on their debts. At any time there was thus a substantial amount of private foreign funds in London, Paris, and Berlin representing the unutilized proceeds of flotations in these centers and funds accumulated for debt service; and the totals were always shifting.[37] The volume of these balances and their fluctuations were not likely to have been significantly influenced by interest-rate differentials or exchange-rate movements.

Mention must also be made of the movements of private short-term capital associated with the working of the commercial-bank-managed gold-exchange-standard systems maintained before 1914 in Canada, Australia, and New Zealand. No central bank existed in any of these countries, and the commercial banks held their reserves partly in the form of balances abroad—mainly in New York in the case of Canada, and in London in the case of Australia and New Zealand—and partly in the form of gold (or Treasury notes convertible into gold) at home. The monetary units of all three countries were defined in terms of gold; commercial bank notes (and Treasury notes where they existed) were convertible into gold on demand; and gold could be freely exported and imported. Except for Australia, gold coin circulated among the public to only a limited extent and, whether circulating or used as bank reserves, consisted mainly of British and, in the case of Canada, American coin. In fact, New Zealand had no mint at all before 1914; and Canada and Australia minted their own gold coins only from 1908 and 1909, respectively. Almost all gold mined in these countries was shipped abroad as an ordinary commodity.

While the institutional arrangements differed somewhat from country to country, the monetary systems in their external aspects worked in essentially the same way in all three cases. Shifts in balances of payments were reflected mainly in changes in the volume of commercial-bank balances abroad which, in an accommodating manner, rose when the balance of payments was in surplus and declined when it was in deficit. Monetary gold, to the extent that it was imported or

[37] All this applies equally to the much larger volume of balances held or accumulated by foreign *government* borrowers. But since such balances were officially owned, their fluctuations involved *official* short-term capital movements according to the definition used here.

47

exported, moved predominantly as a result of changes in the banks' needs for cash reserves at home and to meet domestic gold-circulation requirements if any, and not as a direct result of changes in the balance of payments. Exchange rates in each case were kept within narrow limits of parity, as defined by the gold contents of the respective monetary units, not by gold movements but by commercial-bank purchases and sales of foreign exchange. Apart from the fact that the foreign-exchange reserves were held by the commercial banks,[38] these gold-exchange-standard systems operated in actual practice like many of the officially-managed ones discussed earlier.[39]

Finally, the pre-1914 period witnessed a variety of "abnormal" short-term capital movements associated with capital flight and destabilizing exchange speculation. Although such movements never approached in importance the "hot-money" movements that occurred thereafter, they appear to have been of greater magnitude and frequency than is customarily believed. Discussion of these pre-1914 movements is reserved for a later section.

The foregoing outline of the major kinds and motivations of private short-term capital movements in the period before World War I points up the variety of these movements and of the factors influencing them. While short-term interest-rate differentials and movements of exchange rates within the gold points played a causal role of great importance, it is clear from the discussion that by no means all of these movements could be explained in such terms. Moreover, even when these factors should, in principle at least, have been the determining ones, institutional arrangements or preferences often played the decisive role. For example, international short-term borrowers would often turn to the

[38] While the governments of these countries also undoubtedly held some balances abroad from time to time as a result of their foreign long-term borrowing operations, such balances were not used for purposes of exchange stabilization.

[39] For detailed analyses of the Canadian, Australian, and New Zealand monetary systems, see J. Viner, *Canada's Balance of International Indebtedness, 1900-1913* (Cambridge, Mass., 1924), pp. 153ff.; and A. H. Tocker, "The Monetary Standards of New Zealand and Australia," *Economic Journal*, December 1924. Similar features characterized the monetary systems of many of the smaller overseas British territories. South Africa, however, does not seem to have fallen quite so clearly into this general category. For gold played a much more significant role there in the reserves of the commercial banks and in currency circulation; and monetary gold movements were an important adjusting item in the balance of payments. And one writer has stated that there is no evidence "that it was customary for the banks to allow large London balances to be built up and left abroad." See D. W. Gilbert, "The Economic Effects of the Gold Discoveries upon South Africa," *Quarterly Journal of Economics*, August 1933, p. 555 and *passim*.

market or markets where they had long-standing relationships with the lenders or other ties, even if the funds could at times have been had elsewhere at somewhat lower cost. The availability of funds, moreover, was frequently as important as their cost or yield in determining the volume and direction of international movements of short-term funds.

## A Note on Statistics of Pre-1914 Private Short-term Capital Movements

As suggested earlier, the statistical approach to be used here will be that of working directly with data on private short-term capital movements, where such are available at all. As such, it is a modest supplement to the indirect but much more ambitious approach of Morgenstern and Neisser.

Ideally, the construction of a series of private short-term capital movements into and out of a given country would require the availability of statistical data over a period of years on: (a) the total short-term foreign assets held by the commercial banks and other private institutions and parties resident in that country; and (b) the total short-term liabilities to *private* non-residents of *all* institutions (private and official alike), firms, and persons resident in that country.[40] Only for a few, and for the most part relatively unimportant, countries before 1914 does an approximation to this statistical ideal exist.

Published statistics in this field are extremely limited and are confined exclusively to the commercial banks of a small number of countries. Consolidated balance sheets of commercial-banking systems before 1914, where such are available at all, rarely separated out foreign short-term assets and liabilities from other balance-sheet items. Such a separation is available for Finland, Sweden, and Canada, which provide the most comprehensive and continuous series of private short-term capital movements for the pre-1914 period. Similar but much less satisfactory published series exist for Norwegian, Russian, Austrian, and Swiss commercial banks, these being either incomplete in coverage or relating to only a limited number of years. In a number of other countries, certain *individual* commercial banks regularly reported foreign items separately on their own balance sheets, but, except for Denmark, it proved impossible to derive from them a representative series, since the reporting banks in question constituted only a small part of the commercial-banking system of the countries concerned.

In an effort to obtain further statistical series relating to short-term

[40] This of course follows from the definition of private short-term capital movements noted earlier. See *supra*, pp. 5-6.

foreign assets and liabilities before 1914, I contacted leading commercial banks and other important financial institutions in a substantial number of Western European countries and in the United States. Except for a certain measure of success in France and Norway, the results proved almost wholly negative. Particularly disappointing, although not entirely unexpected, was my inability to get relevant statistics from any of the leading commercial banks and other financial institutions in Great Britain, the United States, and Germany. My queries met with the responses that the records in question had been destroyed or were otherwise unavailable, or that it was impossible from existing records to separate out foreign from domestic short-term assets or liabilities, or that the amount of time and effort needed to assemble the relevant statistics would be too great a burden on the staffs of the institutions concerned. Relevant data were obtained from a few of the smaller banks in at least one of these countries, but they constituted far too limited a sample to be of any use.

We are left, then, with about half a dozen series of sufficient coverage and duration to justify their examination for whatever light they might throw on the pattern of private short-term capital movements before 1914. All of them, as we shall see, are subject to distinct limitations from an analytical point of view.

## The Scandinavian Countries

The series relating to the four Scandinavian countries may conveniently be analyzed together because of the broad similarities in the economic and financial structures of these countries and in the patterns of their economic development and balances of payments. All four countries were essentially export economies undergoing a rapid rate of economic growth based primarily upon large-scale long-term capital imports from abroad; all were continuously on a gold basis, with gold-exchange-standard features, from the mid-1870's on; all had central banks and developed commercial-banking systems operating in a framework of underdeveloped money markets; and all were dependent upon the leading money markets of Western Europe, mainly Germany, England, and France, for long- and short-term capital.

The best of the four series are those relating to Finland and Sweden. For Finland we have monthly data of the foreign short-term assets and liabilities of the commercial-banking system as a whole from 1887 on.[41]

[41] The monthly data were compiled many years ago by the Institute for Economic Research of the Bank of Finland, which kindly put them at my disposal.

The Swedish data are equally comprehensive in coverage, but are available only on an annual (year-end) basis, dating from as far back as 1861.[42] Series of private short-term capital movements for these two countries can readily be obtained by taking the changes in the net foreign assets (or liabilities) in each case.

Comparable data for all Norwegian commercial banks are available on an annual (year-end) basis only from 1907,[43] but I was able to get annual (year-end) series, dating from 1880, for the foreign short-term assets and liabilities of two of the larger Norwegian banks.[44] A comparison of the combined net foreign assets or liabilities of these two banks with those of all the banks after 1907 revealed that, while the former were only a relatively small part of the latter, the two totals tended to move in the same direction from year to year. On the assumption that this similarity of movement also prevailed before 1907, we may use the annual changes in the total for the two banks as an index of the direction of the annual net flow of private short-term capital into and out of Norway as recorded on the books of the commercial-banking system as a whole.

In the case of Denmark, year-end data going back to 1885 were available to me only for the foreign short-term assets of the three biggest commercial banks.[45] Fortunately for our purpose, virtually all of the foreign short-term assets of the Danish commercial banks as a whole were concentrated in these three banks.[46] On the other hand, data for foreign short-term liabilities were available to me for only one of these three banks, and I have consequently decided to work from the assets side alone and to assume that changes in these assets were an index of the direction of the annual net flow of private short-term capital into and out of Denmark.

---

Only parts of the data have been previously published, in various Finnish journals and books. However, the year-end data, from 1885 on, can be found in the *Annuaire Statistique de Finlande* (Helsinki, 1918), pp. 320-323.

[42] *Sveriges Riksbank, 1668-1924*, Vol. 5 (Stockholm, 1931), pp. 178-185.

[43] Central Bureau of Statistics of Norway, *Statistiske Oversikter, 1948* (Oslo, 1948), pp. 316-317.

[44] The Norske Creditbank and the Bergens Privatbank.

[45] The Danske Landmandsbank, the Privatbanken i Kobenhaven, and the Kobenhavens Handelsbank. The statistics were compiled and kindly made available to me by Dr. Helmer D. Nielsen of Copenhagen.

[46] For example, in the year 1913-1914, the foreign short-term assets of these three banks amounted to 42.5 million kroner, as compared with 45.1 million for all Danish commercial banks. See the Danish *Statistisk Aarbog*, 1914, pp. 106-111. Figures for selected earlier years made available to me by Dr. Nielsen reveal the same thing.

The series for the four countries relate only to the net or gross foreign short-term assets of the commercial banks. They thus exclude the assets and liabilities of other private parties, except to the extent that these were held or assumed by the commercial banks themselves and thus reported under their own. The amounts of such assets and liabilities excluded, especially the latter, may well have been substantial.[47]

Little is known about the composition of the foreign assets and liabilities of the commercial banks in these countries. At best one can make only qualitative judgments. The published statistics usually broke down assets only into holdings of foreign bills and claims on foreign correspondents, while there was no breakdown for liabilities at all. Foreign bills presumably included bills drawn on foreign institutions and importers by bank customers and discounted with the banks, as well as bills purchased by the banks on foreign money markets. Claims on foreign correspondents must have consisted primarily of deposits held abroad by the banks for their own account and that of their customers, as well as funds put out on loan on foreign markets. The absence of money markets in the four countries made it necessary for the banks to seek foreign outlets for the acquisition of liquid income-earning assets as secondary reserves. The banks' foreign liabilities undoubtedly consisted mainly of acceptance obligations on trade account incurred on behalf of local importers and of short-term borrowings on their own account from foreign correspondents. It is unlikely that foreigners held any substantial amounts of deposits in these banks.[48]

A major limitation of the data for purposes of statistical analysis is that they provide no information as to the geographical distribution of the reported short-term foreign assets and liabilities of the commercial banks concerned.[49] It is thus impossible to obtain series of the net flow of short-term funds to and from individual foreign countries and

[47] To the extent that the foreign short-term liabilities of the commercial banks were owing to foreign *official* institutions, changes in the amount of such liabilities would not involve a *private* short-term capital movement. But the amounts so involved must have been negligible.

[48] On the other hand, one writer has stated that French banks maintained "large balances on deposit with Swedish banks," on the basis of which the latter made loans to Swedish industry. See R. Cameron, *France and the Economic Development of Europe, 1800-1914* (Princeton, 1961), p. 491. I suspect, however, that he may have really meant French short-term credits to, rather than deposits in, Swedish banks.

[49] The bulk of these assets and liabilities undoubtedly represented claims on and debts to England, Germany, and France. Russia may also have been a significant short-term debtor and creditor in the case of Finland.

to make appropriate use of related series, such as exchange rates and foreign short-term interest rates, that might otherwise have been relevant. We will have to do what we can with the global figures.

Charts 7 and 8 plot the stock of net foreign short-term assets (or liabilities) of the commercial banks in each of the four countries[50] on the basis of the data described above, along with the stock of reserves (gold and foreign exchange) of the respective central banks.[51] The gross foreign short-term assets and liabilities of the Swedish commercial banks are also shown separately because of their relatively large size in relation to the net figures. The net foreign assets of *all* Norwegian commercial banks, data for which are available for 1907-1913, are likewise plotted in order to enable a comparison of their movements with those of the two commercial banks. The monthly data for Finland, both for the commercial banks and the central bank, have been seasonally adjusted. Finally, arrows are inserted at the bottom of each panel in the two charts to indicate the reference dates of business-cycle peaks and troughs in each of the four countries.[52]

The foreign assets of the Finnish, Swedish, and Norwegian commercial banks were usually larger, as the charts indicate, than their foreign liabilities. During the later years of the period, however, the banks frequently ran net foreign short-term debtor positions because of sharp upsurges in their foreign liabilities, these being most marked in the case of Sweden. In each of the four countries the stock of central-bank reserves showed a pronounced upward trend over the period. There was no similarly marked upward trend, however, in the net foreign short-term assets of the commercial banks,[53] on which the initial impact

[50] For Denmark, as already noted, the figures refer only to *gross* foreign short-term assets.

[51] The statistics of the gold and foreign-exchange reserves of the central banks have been taken from their balance sheets. I have adjusted the reserves of the Bank of Sweden for its borrowings of *foreign exchange* (as contrasted with Swedish kroner) from the Swedish National Debt Office in 1899-1902 and 1907-1908. Similarly, I have adjusted the reserves of the Bank of Finland for its special borrowings from foreign banks in 1892-1893, 1908-1909, and 1913.

[52] For the sources of the cyclical-turning-point dates for Finland, Norway, and Denmark, see Bloomfield, *Monetary Policy*, p. 29n. For Sweden, see L. Jörberg, *Growth and Fluctuations of Swedish Industry, 1869-1912* (Stockholm, 1961), pp. 218-219.

[53] To be sure, the gross foreign short-term assets of the Danish commercial banks showed a pronounced upward trend, but if data for their foreign liabilities were available the net figures would probably show no such trend. This conclusion suggests itself from an examination of the annual foreign liabilities of the one Danish commercial bank for which I have such data. While foreign assets were usually larger than liabilities, both rose by about the same amount over the period.

53

**CHART 7**

## SHORT-TERM FOREIGN ASSETS OF COMMERCIAL BANKS AND RESERVES OF CENTRAL BANK

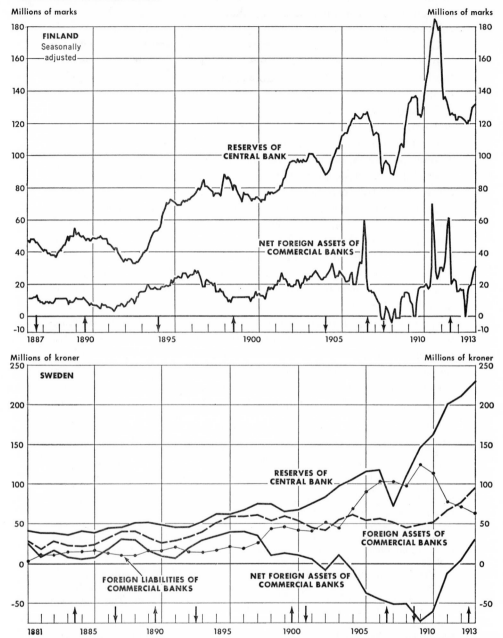

Note: Arrows on the bottom of each panel indicate dates of reference cycle peaks and troughs.

CHART 8

## SHORT-TERM FOREIGN ASSETS OF COMMERCIAL BANKS AND RESERVES OF CENTRAL BANK

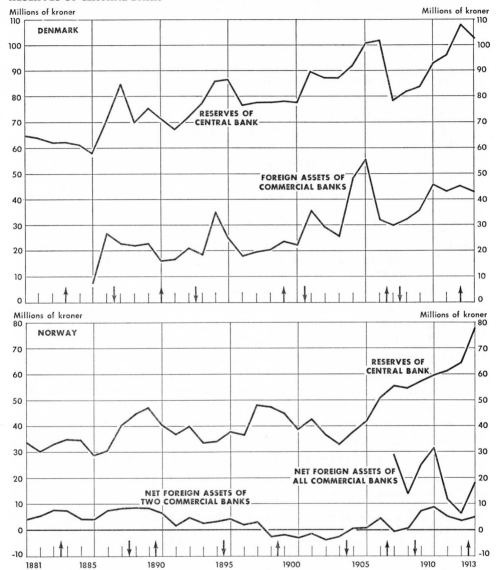

Note: Arrows on the bottom of each panel indicate dates of reference cycle peaks and troughs.

of balance-of-payments swings mainly fell, indicating that over the period as a whole these banks must have passed on to their respective central banks the bulk of their net acquisitions of foreign exchange.

Of immediate interest is the relation between the *changes* in commercial-bank net foreign assets (i.e., the net movement of private short-term capital) and in central-bank reserves from year to year and, as in the case of Finland, from month to month. According to the customary view of the pre-1914 gold standard, private short-term capital movements tended to reduce or substitute for, rather than to cause or accentuate, movements of official gold and foreign-exchange reserves. More specifically, private short-term capital flows were supposed to have usually the same, rather than the opposite, balance-of-payments sign as changes in official reserves. Thus a net inflow of private short-term funds (plus sign) would tend to be associated with a decrease in official reserves (plus sign), and a net outflow (minus sign) with an increase in official reserves (minus sign). Our statistical series, imperfect though they might be, enable us to test the validity of this view for the four countries in question.

The necessary data for this purpose can be derived from the statistics underlying Charts 7 and 8. Chart 9 plots, for each of the four countries, the annual *changes* in the stock of net foreign short-term assets of the commercial banks[54]—that is, the annual net movement of private short-term capital[55]—and the annual *changes* in the stock of central-bank gold and foreign-exchange reserves. The data are simply the first differences in the relevant stock series used in Charts 7 and 8, after adjustment for trend where necessary. In the case of Finland, however, we plot the first differences in the annual averages of the monthly data (again after adjustment for trend where necessary), instead of in the monthly data themselves. Plus signs in Chart 9 are of course minus signs from the viewpoint of balance-of-payments accounting, and vice versa.[56] Thus, for example, a plus sign for changes in the stock of com-

[54] For Denmark the changes relate to the stock of *gross* foreign short-term assets of the commercial banks.

[55] We use the term "movement of private short-term capital" as a short expression for the movement that was recorded on the books of the commercial banks. As noted above, not all private short-term capital flows showed up on the balance sheets of the commercial banks. And in the cases of Denmark and Norway the data do not even give a complete picture of the movements that were reflected on the banks' books, for reasons already given.

[56] So far as the changes in central-bank reserves are concerned, this involves the assumption, which is believed to be reasonably correct, that the changes in the gold component of those reserves were due entirely to balance-of-payments trans-

CHART 9

## CHANGES IN NET (OR GROSS) FOREIGN ASSETS OF
## COMMERCIAL BANKS AND IN RESERVES OF CENTRAL BANK

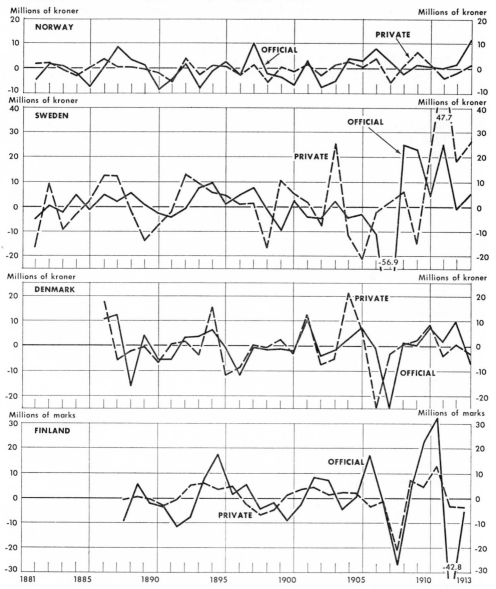

Note: Underlying series have been adjusted for trend where necessary.

mercial-bank net foreign assets represents a net outflow of short-term capital, and a minus sign a net inflow.

To test whether private short-term capital movements were characteristically equilibrating or not, we simply counted the number of years in which the items in the two series, in the case of each country, both had the same sign, that is, were both on the same side of the zero line. For Finland we used the same procedure with the *monthly* data as well, experimenting with various lagged relationships; the greatest proportion of the same signs was found when the changes in central-bank reserves were lagged four months behind the changes in the net foreign assets of the commercial banks. The results are summarized in Table II.

TABLE II

Sign Correlations: Changes in Commercial-Bank
Net Foreign Assets and in
Central-Bank Reserves, Scandinavian Countries[a]

| Country | Period | Number of Observations | Number of Times Both Showed Same Sign[b] | Percentage of Same Signs |
|---------|--------|------------------------|------------------------------------------|--------------------------|
| | | *Annual Data* | | |
| Denmark | 1886-1913 | 28 | 21 | 75.0 |
| Sweden | 1881-1913 | 33 | 23 | 69.7 |
| Norway | 1881-1913 | 33 | 22 | 66.7 |
| Finland | 1888-1913 | 26[c] | 20 | 76.9 |
| | | *Monthly Data*[d] | | |
| Finland | Feb. 1887– Dec. 1913 | 319 | 190.5 | 59.7 |

[a] Underlying series have been adjusted for trend where necessary.
[b] Zero change counted as one-half.
[c] Annual averages of monthly data.
[d] Seasonally adjusted. Central-bank reserves lagged by four months.

The sign correlations are in each case significant. They are highly significant in the cases of Finland (the annual though not the monthly data) and Denmark.[57] Despite the limitations of the series of private

actions, and not in part merely to changes in private domestic gold holdings or in internal gold-coin circulation.

[57] Coefficients of correlation were also computed for each of the five pairs of series. The coefficients (reading down in Table II) were, respectively, .4138, .2435, .3490, .5953, and .1408. Only the fourth of these coefficients (that relating to the changes in the annual averages of monthly Finnish data) was significant. Correlation coefficients were also computed for the monthly Finnish data with central-bank reserves lagged all the way up to ten months. None of the results was

short-term capital movements and the shortcomings (in the cases of Sweden, Norway, and Denmark) of year-end data, these findings give support to the view that changes in commercial-bank net foreign assets had a tendency to reduce rather than to increase the size of changes in the central-bank reserves of the four countries in question, that is, to behave in an equilibrating fashion. Whether or not other categories of private short-term capital movements not included in our series tended to behave in the same manner is not known.

The results might perhaps be stated in this way. When during a given period the commercial banks in any of these countries were on balance acquiring foreign exchange as a result of transactions with their customers, they would tend in effect to turn part of it over to the central bank,[58] but retain part themselves (and/or use it to repay some of their outstanding short-term foreign borrowings). This would result both in rising central-bank reserves and in rising commercial-bank net foreign assets during the period in question, i.e., an increase in central-bank reserves would be accompanied by an equilibrating net outflow of private short-term capital.[59] Conversely, when the commercial banks were on balance losing foreign exchange through transactions with their customers, they would tend to meet part of those losses by obtaining foreign exchange or gold from the central bank and part by drawing down their own foreign balances (and/or by borrowing at short-term abroad). As a consequence, the decline in central-bank reserves during the period in question would tend to be accompanied by an equilibrating net inflow of private short-term capital. This is of course a description of a (likely) pattern of events, not an explanation of that pattern.

Although the level of the commercial banks' net foreign assets was subject to day-to-day fluctuations under the impact of changes in their customers' foreign payments and receipts, more fundamentally it depended upon how large or small a volume of such assets the banks

---

significant, and only the six months' lag yielded a higher coefficient (.2045) than that for the four-months' lag given above.

[58] More specifically, the excess of commercial-bank purchases over sales of foreign exchange would tend to depress the price of foreign exchange in terms of the local currency until it became profitable to import gold for sale to the central bank or necessary for the central bank to buy foreign exchange to prevent the local currency from moving to the gold import point.

[59] With regard to the monthly data at least, we would expect a time lag here (and also when the banks were losing foreign exchange). This helps to explain why in the case of the monthly Finnish data the best sign correlations were obtained when changes in central-bank reserves were lagged (by four months) behind changes in commercial-bank net foreign assets.

wished to maintain. For the choice was always open to them to alter the size of those assets by buying or selling foreign exchange or gold from or to their central banks or by short-term borrowings abroad (or repayments of such borrowings). This choice, and thus the level and fluctuations of their foreign net assets, was influenced by a variety of factors, including: the relation between short-term interest rates abroad and central-bank discount rates at home (which influenced the banks' decision as to whether and to what extent to meet their growing reserve needs at home by borrowing at the central bank, on the one hand, or by repatriating foreign assets and/or by short-term borrowing abroad, on the other);[60] expected movements of exchange rates within the gold points; the pattern of the banks' expected future payments and receipts abroad (which influenced the size of the working balances they believed necessary to maintain abroad during given future periods of time); the size of their reserve needs at home; and many other considerations.[61]

In view of the fact that the series on the net foreign assets of the commercial banks are on a year-end basis (except for Finland) and are not broken down into the major foreign countries concerned, and in view of the absence of data for many of the relevant variables, the possibility of statistically explaining the changes that actually occurred in these assets seems definitely limited. A few simple correlations, however, were made with respect to Finland. Working in all cases with annual averages of monthly data, we correlated the changes in the excess of the discount rate of the Bank of Finland over the simple average of short-term interest rates in London, Berlin, and Paris with (a) changes in the net foreign assets of the Finnish commercial banks, on the one hand, and (b) changes in the *ratio* of these assets to the sum of these assets and reserves of the Bank of Finland, on the other. One would expect a tendency towards inverse correlation in each case. The correlation coefficients were —.4853 and —.4573, respectively, neither of which, however, was significant.

[60] The importance of this factor for Sweden has been noted by Karin Kock, *A Study of Interest Rates* (London, 1929), pp. 188-189. According to Miss Kock, when the discount rate of the Swedish central bank was low compared with interest rates obtainable abroad, the commercial banks preferred rediscounting to selling foreign exchange to the central bank, and when the discount rate was relatively high they were anxious not to hold more foreign balances than was necessary.

[61] For a detailed analysis—although in a somewhat different historical and institutional context—of the factors affecting the amount of balances held abroad by commercial banks and the fluctuations in these balances over time, see P. W. Bell, *The Sterling Area in the Post-War World* (Oxford, 1956), pp. 94ff.

In growing export economies, such as the four countries under consideration here, where business-cycle fluctuations were mainly imported from abroad, one would expect the aggregate of central-bank reserves plus commercial-bank net foreign assets to tend to rise during periods of business-cycle expansion and to fall (or to rise at a slower rate) during periods of contraction. Since central-bank reserves were in each case much larger than the net foreign assets of the commercial banks, one might expect such a pattern to show up also, and perhaps even more clearly, in the behavior of the former series alone.

A simple means of testing this would be to compute "indexes of conformity" for the relevant series along the lines of the technique of the National Bureau of Economic Research.[62] A difficulty presents itself, however, in that the Swedish, Norwegian, and Danish series are on a year-end basis, whereas the reference dates for these countries (indicated by arrows on Charts 7 and 8) are annual and have had to be centered in the middle of the relevant years, except where the dates were given as falling within a two-year period, in which case they have been assumed to be at the end of the first of the two years in question. For these three countries, then, we will have to rely on the cruder procedure of a simple inspection of the charts, supplemented where necessary by use of absolute deviations from trend, in an effort to determine whether the relevant series tended to conform with the waves in general business activity. This difficulty did not present itself for Finland, where the data are monthly, although here, too, the reference dates are annual only.

Despite these limitations, central-bank reserves in Finland, Norway, and Sweden, as expected, tended to conform positively to the cycle. For Finland the conformity indexes were +100 for reference expansions, +33 for reference contractions, and +67 for full cycles, indicating that the series was a well conforming one. For Denmark, however, central-bank reserves seemed to exhibit an inverse conformity to business cycles, even after the foreign assets of the commercial banks were added in. This was an unexpected result, which might well have been different if we had had monthly data to work with.

The Finnish, Danish, and Swedish series on the foreign assets of the commercial banks appear to reflect a tendency towards *inverse* conformity to their respective business cycles. No consistent cyclical tendency seems apparent for Norway. The conformity indexes for Finland

[62] A. F. Burns and W. C. Mitchell, *Measuring Business Cycles* (New York, 1946), pp. 31-33.

were —50 for reference expansions, —33 for reference contractions, and —33 for full cycles. This result is not of course necessarily inconsistent with our earlier finding that changes in Finnish commercial-bank net foreign assets tended to move in the same direction as changes in reserves of the Bank of Finland on a monthly and annual basis.

## Canada

The monthly returns of the Canadian chartered banks provide detailed statistics, especially after 1900, of the foreign short-term claims and liabilities of the Canadian banking system before World War I. Unfortunately, the use to which these statistics can be put for our purpose is very limited.[63]

For the period 1880-1913 continuous monthly data are available for the amounts due from and due to banks and banking correspondents in Great Britain, on the one hand, and in other foreign countries (known to be predominantly the United States), on the other. In addition, commencing in July 1900, there are available separate monthly series pertaining to the banks' call and short loans elsewhere than in Canada (again known to be predominantly the United States), as well as their current loans and their deposit liabilities elsewhere than in Canada (a significant part of which is believed to represent the business of branches of Canadian banks in Newfoundland and Caribbean countries). The relation between the various series before and after July 1900 is not clear;[64] and the exact geographical breakdown of these series, except for those pertaining explicitly to Great Britain, is not available.

The net balances due from banks and banking correspondents abroad, plus call and short loans elsewhere than in Canada, constituted, as Viner has pointed out, the secondary reserves (or "outside reserves")

[63] The statistics are conveniently brought together, along with others, in C. A. Curtis, "Statistics of Banking," in *Statistical Contributions to Canadian Economic History*, by C. A. Curtis and K. W. Taylor (Toronto, 1931), Vol. I.

[64] For example, it is not clear how call and short loans outside Canada were treated in the statistics before July 1900. According to Curtis' descriptive notes (*op.cit.*, p. 12), these loans before July 1900 were part of the balance reported under sums due from banks in foreign countries. On the other hand, another writer has asserted that these loans were reported under *domestic* short-term loans and were thus not part of the "due from" series at all. See P. Hartland, "Canadian Balance of Payments since 1863," in *Trends in the American Economy in the Nineteenth Century*, National Bureau of Economic Research (Princeton, 1960), p. 730. Indeed, Miss Hartland makes rough annual estimates of the changes in total Canadian call loans abroad from 1880 to 1899.

of the Canadian banks. These reserves fluctuated broadly in keeping with the fluctuations in the Canadian balance of payments. Gold was imported (or exported) by the banks only when and to the extent needed to keep their cash-reserve ratios in Canada at customary or desired levels. There was no hand-to-hand circulation of gold as money. The Canadian monetary system before 1914 was in effect a gold- (or U.S. dollar-) exchange standard operated, in the absence of a central bank, by the chartered banks themselves.

On the basis of the data described above, we have put together two monthly series which it is hoped gives a not too inaccurate picture, at least after July 1900, of the "outside reserves" of the Canadian banks in Great Britain and in the United States, respectively. The first, covering the whole period 1880-1913, was obtained simply by taking the difference between the amounts due from and due to banks and banking correspondents in Great Britain. The second is broken into two parts. One, covering the period 1880-1899 inclusive, was similarly obtained by taking the difference between the amounts due from and due to banks and banking correspondents in other foreign countries. The other part, dating from July 1900 to December 1913, includes both these net balances *and* call and short loans elsewhere than in Canada. This procedure involves the assumptions among others that *all* call and short loans elsewhere than in Canada were placed in the United States and also that the net balances due from foreign countries other than Great Britain applied exclusively to the United States. The first of these assumptions is by far the more important in view of the relative size of these loans; but judging from the statements of Viner and others as to the predominance of Canadian call loans in New York as compared with London,[65] it probably does not depart too seriously from the actual facts. On the other hand, if call loans were *not* reported in the net-balances series before July 1900, then the series on New York funds before that date understates the actual totals.[66]

The two series, whatever their limitations might be, have been seasonally adjusted and are plotted in Chart 10. It is at once evident that the great bulk of the outside reserves of the Canadian banking system was held at all times in the United States. The difference in the size of the reserves held in each of the two countries became especially marked after 1900, with the great increase in the aggregate of these reserves coinciding with the period of accelerated economic growth in

[65] See Viner, *Canada's Balance*, pp. 91, 164, 177, and *passim*.
[66] See footnote 64, p. 62.

Canada and large-scale borrowings from abroad. By far the larger part of that increase took the form of call loans in New York, which were also the most volatile component of the total. Net balances from banks and banking correspondents in the United States (and in Great Britain) showed no marked increase after 1900. The outside reserve position of Canadian banks vis-a-vis London was, as the chart indicates, very frequently that of a net debtor during the period as a whole; in fact, net creditor positions were consistently maintained only in the late 1890's and in 1908-1912. On the other hand, the sums due to banks in the United States were at all times only a small or negligible fraction of the sums due from banks in the United States.

The relatively small fluctuations in the net holdings of sterling funds during the period reflected the fact, noted by Viner, that the Canadian banks tended immediately to convert any currently accruing sterling funds, if in excess of the small amounts needed as working balances,

CHART 10

**CANADA: "OUTSIDE RESERVES" OF THE CHARTERED BANKS**

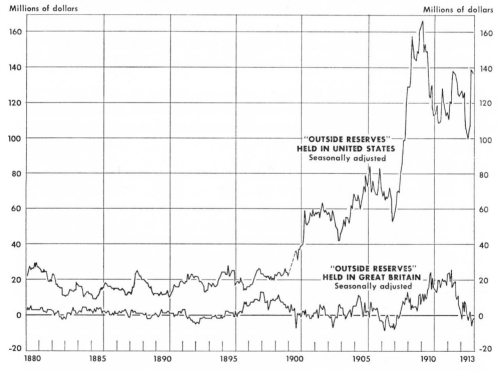

into U.S. dollar funds (or gold). This procedure served the banks' interests in view of the fact that outside reserves in New York could generally earn higher interest rates than in London and could in case of need be converted into gold and brought into Canada overnight with a minimum risk of exchange loss.

It is tempting to examine whether there might have been some systematic relationship between the changes in the proportion of Canada's outside reserves held in the United States and in relative short-term interest rates in New York and London. Canadian banks had the choice of keeping their outside reserves in New York or in London; and we want to determine whether changes in the relative proportions held in the two centers might have been systematically responsive to changes in the relation between interest rates in those centers. To do so, we correlated the monthly changes in the ratio of gross outside reserves held in New York to total gross outside reserves (in New York and London), and the monthly changes in the ratio of the New York call-money rate to the London open-market discount rate (3 months' sterling bank-bill rate).[67] One correlation was made for the period 1880-1899 and the other for the period July 1900 to December 1913, corresponding to the two segments of the series for United States funds. No correlation whatsoever was indicated for either of the two periods. The correlation coefficient for the first period was —.0897 and for the second period worked out to a perfect zero. The results were no better when the changes in the proportion of outside reserves held in the United States were lagged by one month.

*France*

Before 1914 France was a huge creditor on long-term account, with investments abroad exceeded only by those of Great Britain. As an international short-term money market and acceptance center, however, Paris never reached the stage of development of London or even Berlin, but relative to other leading gold-standard countries it unquestionably had very substantial foreign short-term claims and liabilities and was especially important as an international short-term lender.[68]

[67] We used ratios of *gross* outside reserves only because the net outside reserve position of the banks vis-a-vis Great Britain was frequently that of a debtor. Gross outside reserves included the "due from" items and, in the case of the United States after July 1900, call loans. All of the underlying series were seasonally adjusted. For the period 1880-1890 we might have used the United States commercial-paper rate instead of the call-loan rate, but it is very doubtful if this would have significantly altered the final results.

[68] Some writers, however, seem to deny this. For example, Margaret Myers

French banks, as was noted earlier, were lenders at short-term to Germany, Russia, the United States and other countries, especially in the form of purchases of foreign paper *en pension*. At all times they held substantial amounts of foreign bills and of deposits abroad. Kaufmann, in his comprehensive survey of French banking in 1914, referred to the important place held by foreign bills in the portfolios of the deposit banks and noted that London bills were the most eagerly sought after, with German and American paper coming next.[69] French banks also had large deposit and related liabilities to foreigners. Every bank of any importance in developed countries, according to Kaufmann, kept an account with one of the three main deposit banks—the Crédit Lyonnais, the Société Générale, and the Comptoir National d'Escompte.[70] Large balances were also kept with these banks and with the big *banques d'affaires* by foreign governments and business enterprises in connection with their long-term borrowing operations in the Paris market. Especially important, of course, were the balances of the Russian Government to which reference was made earlier.

Detailed statistical information regarding the foreign short-term assets and liabilities of the French banks is not available. Some of the leading banks, however, regularly published their foreign-bill holdings in their annual reports. The statistics of such holdings, on a year-end basis, are available for the Société Générale and the Banque de Paris et des Pays Bas (the largest of the *banques d'affaires*), during the entire period in which we are interested; for the Comptoir National d'Escompte from 1889 to 1903; and for the Crédit Industriel et Commercial (the fourth largest deposit bank) up to 1901. The Banque de Paris et des Pays Bas also reported annually, up to 1905, its other short-term foreign assets, as well as its short-term foreign liabilities, but it was the only French bank to do so.[71]

---

(*Paris as a Financial Center* [New York, 1936], p. 1), states that "Paris neither loaned nor borrowed abroad on short-term for large amounts." Another writer has stated that in the case of France "les mouvements de capitaux à court terme étaient réduits au strict minimum." See J. Malpas, *Les Mouvements Internationaux de Capitaux* (Paris, 1934), pp. 188-189.

[69] Kaufmann, *La Banque en France*, pp. 285-286. See also Coste, *Les Grands Marchés Financiers*, p. 20: "Nos banques détenaient . . . un portefeuille important d'acceptations anglaises et plaçaient des sommes élevées dans les banques étrangères."

[70] Kaufmann, *op.cit.*, pp. 266-267.

[71] The Société Générale reported on its balance sheets an extremely large item, on both the assets and liabilities sides, entitled "comptes de banque a l'étranger et comptes courants divers," but it was impossible to separate out the foreign component.

With the cooperation of the banks concerned, I have been able to get year-end data of the foreign-bill holdings of the Crédit Lyonnais, the largest deposit bank, for the entire period, as well the missing data for the Comptoir National d'Escompte from 1904 to 1913.[72] The missing figures for the Crédit Industriel et Commercial for 1902 to 1913 could not be obtained.[73] It also proved impossible to get data from any of the big deposit banks for their other foreign short-term assets or for their foreign liabilities.

We are left, then, with an annual series from 1880 to 1913 of the foreign-bill holdings of the four leading deposit banks (which had over 75 per cent of total commercial deposits[74]) and the leading *banque d'affaires*. While certain of the other banks, including private banking houses, undoubtedly held some foreign bills also, the sums involved could have been only relatively small. On the other hand, the series covers only the foreign bills held by the metropolitan offices of the banks concerned and not by their overseas branches. To the extent that the foreign bills held by the latter were for the account of the metropolitan offices, they should logically, from a balance-of-payments point of view, have been included in our series, but the relevant data were not available.[75] It is not clear, moreover, whether or to what extent the figures include foreign bills taken by French banks *en pension*, i.e., foreign short-term loans proper, as contrasted with bills purchased in the open market or from their customers. In any case, foreign-bill holdings were only one part of the total short-term foreign assets held by the banks. Other claims on foreigners, including deposits abroad, may well have been considerably larger.[76] In view of these various considerations, it is far from certain that changes in foreign-bill

[72] On the other hand, data could not be obtained for the foreign-bill holdings from 1880 to 1889 of the predecessor of the Comptoir National, the old Comptoir d'Escompte.

[73] The data for 1880 to 1901, however, indicate that the foreign-bill holdings of this institution were relatively very small.

[74] H. D. White, *The French International Accounts, 1880-1913* (Cambridge, Mass., 1933), p. 173.

[75] For two of the banks I have data for the amounts of foreign bills held by their overseas branches, which were sometimes as large as, or larger than, the amounts held by the metropolitan offices. But I do not know exactly what part of these sums represented bills held for the account of the metropolitan offices as contrasted with bills purchased by the branches for their own account.

[76] If we examine the position of the Banque de Paris et des Pays Bas, which is the only bank for which statistics of all foreign short-term claims are available, we find that foreign-bill holdings were usually only a small part of the total. This may not, however, have been representative of the other banks.

holdings moved in the same direction from year to year with changes in aggregate foreign short-term claims of the French banks or, if allowance could also be made for the changes in their short-term foreign liabilities, had the same balance-of-payments sign as the aggregate net movement of short-term capital on banking account as a whole.

Despite these limitations, the series of foreign-bill holdings is plotted in Chart 11. In the lower panel of the chart are also plotted the annual changes in these holdings, after adjustment for trend, and the absolute deviations from trend of annual net imports of gold into France.[77] Arrows are inserted indicating the (monthly) reference dates of cyclical peaks and troughs in France.

The stock of foreign bills rose only moderately before 1895[78] as compared with the sharp increase that took place thereafter. The year-end total, amounting to 554 million francs ($157 million) in 1913 and ranging between 130 to 586 million francs from 1896 to 1913, must understate very considerably the aggregate short-term foreign claims of the French banking system. For example, outstanding short-term loans of French banking establishments to Russian banks and business concerns alone are estimated to have amounted to 500 million francs at the outbreak of World War I,[79] and the total was at times probably higher in earlier years. French loans *en pension* to German banks, some of which may be reflected in our series, were estimated at times, as noted earlier, to have been in excess of one billion francs. In May 1904 the *Economist* estimated that "a little while ago" French holdings of sterling bills alone amounted to £40 million, or approximately one billion francs;[80] yet our series shows total bill holdings of only about 300 million at the end of 1903. Of course, all of these estimates may have been too high to begin with, but even so they lend support to the view that the series used here underestimates materially the aggregate short-term foreign claims of the French banking system.

In view of the tendency for short-term interest rates in France to fluctuate less sharply than rates in the other leading financial centers

[77] We use net gold movements instead of changes in the gold stock of the Bank of France because the latter were heavily influenced by internal gold movements.

[78] Part of the upward bulge in the series in 1889 reflects the inclusion of the holdings of the Comptoir National d'Escompte in that year.

[79] M. W. Bernatzky, "Monetary Policy of the Russian Government During the War," in *Russian Public Finance During the War*, edited by Michelson, Apostol, and Bernatzky (New Haven, 1928), p. 368.

[80] *Economist*, May 21, 1904, p. 858. Doubtless this estimate included the bill holdings of French branches in London, which we exclude.

CHART 11

## FRANCE: FOREIGN BILL HOLDINGS OF COMMERCIAL BANKS AND NET GOLD IMPORTS

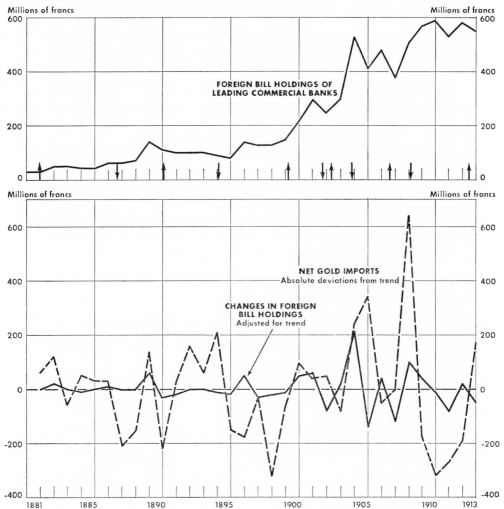

Note: Arrows on bottom of panel indicate dates of reference cycle peaks and troughs.

but to rise and fall with them over the course of the business cycle,[81] one might expect that French holdings of foreign bills (and French short-term foreign loans) would tend to be relatively high in periods of cyclical expansion and relatively low during recessions.[82] But even after allowance for the fact that the series is on a year-end basis, whereas the reference dates for French cycles are monthly, there is no evidence, either by inspecting the upper panel of Chart 11 or by using absolute deviations from trend, of any tendency for foreign-bill holdings to move positively with the cycle. Indeed, in the later part of the period there is even a suggestion of an inverse correlation. On the other hand, the absolute deviations from trend of net gold imports indicate quite clearly that net gold imports tended to move inversely with the cycle.

If the changes in foreign-bill holdings, after adjustment for trend, had usually the same balance-of-payments sign as the aggregate net flow of private short-term capital into and out of France, and if the latter were characteristically equilibrating in character, one would expect a tendency for the former to have the same sign as the absolute deviations from trend of French net gold imports. But a comparison of the signs of the two series, as shown in the lower panel of the chart, indicates no such correlation whatever. Of the 33 observations, the number of times the two series both showed the same sign was only 16, or approximately 50 per cent.

[81] See Morgenstern, *International Financial Transactions*, chapter 3.
[82] See also J. S. Pesmazoglu, "Quelques Aspects Internationaux des Fluctuations Cycliques en France de 1880 à 1913," *Revue d'Economie Politique*, January-February 1951, p. 126.

## IV. INTERNATIONAL SHORT-TERM CREDITOR-
## DEBTOR POSITIONS

In the absence of satisfactory series relating to private short-term capital movements for countries other than those examined above, we will bring together what little statistical information exists regarding the international short-term creditor-debtor position[1] of certain of these countries just before World War I. Where possible, we will also refer to the major components and geographical distribution of the short-term foreign assets and liabilities in question and the broad trend of these items over time.

### Great Britain

In view of the central role of Great Britain in the pre-1914 gold standard, it is particularly unfortunate that there is an almost complete lack of statistics of short-term capital movements for that country.[2] The availability of such statistics would, among other things, have enabled a direct testing of the validity of certain widely held views or dogmas regarding the pattern of these movements in the British balance of payments and their relation to policy of the Bank of England and the functioning of the gold-standard system.

Before 1914 Great Britain was the world's largest (gross) short-term creditor. Its short-term foreign assets consisted primarily of acceptance claims on foreigners representing commercial and finance bills that had been accepted by London houses on their behalf. It is believed that in 1913 the total of sterling bank acceptances outstanding amounted to some £350 million ($1,715 million),[3] but it is not known exactly what part of this figure consisted of acceptances made on behalf of for-

[1] By the net international short-term creditor-debtor position of a country we mean the relation between its aggregate (private and official) holdings of short-term claims on foreigners and its aggregate short-term liabilities to foreigners (private parties and official institutions alike). Gold holdings are excluded from the assets side.

[2] A number of estimates have been made of Britain's balance of payments on an annual basis before 1914, but short-term capital movements have always been grouped in the residual item along with the net flow of long-term capital and/or errors and omissions. See e.g., A. E. Imlah, "British Balance of Payments and Export of Capital, 1816-1913," *Economic History Review*, 2nd Series, Vol. V (1952) No. 2, especially pp. 237-239. It would be hazardous to try to derive a reliable series of short-term capital movements by subtracting from the residual item direct estimates of Britain's long-term capital movements, such as have been made by C. K. Hobson.

[3] See footnote 18, p. 40.

eigners as contrasted with British residents. One writer has ventured the guess that perhaps two-thirds of the total represented debts payable by foreigners;[4] in any case the fraction was a substantial one.[5]

Other foreign short-term claims held by Britain in the years just before World War I were probably relatively small. Many commentators referred to the fact that the amount of foreign bills held by the London joint-stock banks and the public generally were all but negligible,[6] although some such bills were held in the portfolios of the London branches of foreign banks.[7] British banks probably kept no substantial amount of deposits abroad as working balances in view of the fact that the great bulk of Britain's international transactions was settled in sterling. On the other hand, British holdings of short-term notes placed in London by foreign governments and corporations may, as noted earlier, have been relatively sizeable. Nothing is known as to the magnitude of other British short-term claims on foreigners, including bank overdrafts to foreign customers and funds put out on loan on foreign money markets.

On the other side of Britain's international short-term balance sheet, the picture is even more obscure. Unquestionably, England had large short-term liabilities to the rest of the world, mainly in the form of foreign holdings of sterling bills, short loans to the discount market, and deposits in London banks,[8] but only scattered estimates of these liabilities for isolated dates are available, and it is not even clear how comprehensive these are supposed to be. Thus, for example, Giffen estimated in 1901 that about £50 million was held in London by foreign bankers

[4] E. V. Morgan, *Studies in British Financial Policy, 1914-25* (London, 1952), p. 8. Hartley Withers estimated the amount of London's short-term claims on foreigners in 1909 at between £150-200 million, as quoted by J. Schumpeter, *Business Cycles* (New York, 1939), Vol. II, p. 673.

[5] See J. M. Keynes, "War and the Financial System, August 1914," *Economic Journal,* September 1914, p. 466; and *Report of the Committee on Finance and Industry* (London, 1931), p. 148. Just before 1914 London acceptance credits to Germany alone amounted to as much as £70 million, according to R. H. Brand, *War and National Finance* (London, 1921), p. 25.

[6] See, e.g., R. H. I. Palgrave, *Bank Rate and the Money Market* (London, 1903), p. 212: "there are very few, it might almost be said there are hardly any, foreign bills held in England." See also G. Clare, *A Money Market Primer and Key to the Exchanges,* Second Edition (London, 1920), p. 93.

[7] W. F. Spalding, "The Foreign Branch Banks in England," *Economic Journal,* December 1912, p. 621.

[8] Including the Bank of England. According to J. A. Todd, *The Mechanism of Exchange,* Fifth Edition (London, 1946), pp. 80-81: "many foreigners of all kinds, from crowned heads downwards . . . kept accounts with the Bank of England."

and merchants that was liable to be called at short notice.[9] The *Statist* in 1902 estimated that £60 million of short-term money was employed in London by the continent alone, quite apart from American and colonial funds.[10] In 1904 Schuster put the amount of sterling *bills* held abroad at between £50-100 million, in addition to other foreign balances held in London.[11] Although I have been unable to locate any later estimates, it would appear from the contemporary discussion that in the years just before 1914 the total of Britain's short-term foreign liabilities must have grown sharply. The largest holders of short-term claims on England were undoubtedly France, Germany, Japan, India, Russia, and the United States.

It has been customary to assume or to assert that before 1914 Great Britain was a large *net* international creditor on short-term account. In the words of the Macmillan Report, Britain had "sight claims on the rest of the world much greater than those of the rest of the world on it."[12] This probably was the general rule, but statistical or other evidence advanced in support of this view has never been particularly impressive. Indeed, the Macmillan Report itself in a later passage appears to be somewhat less affirmative by stating that before 1914 London's short-term foreign position was "probably well balanced" and that, if the Bank of England's gold holdings were added in, Britain's liquid international assets "were believed, as a rule, to be at least equal to and sometimes substantially in excess of its short-term international liabilities."[13] And Keynes had a year earlier surmised that "in the nineteenth century London's position . . . was a more balanced one than we were then taught to believe, and that foreign short-term funds employed in London were not far short of the volume of foreign business financed through British holdings of sterling bills drawn in respect of trade which was not specifically British."[14] More probably, with its short-term assets not differing greatly in size from its liabilities, Britain

[9] Sir Robert Giffen, "The Expenditure of National Capital," *Journal of the Institute of Bankers*, June 1901, p. 258.

[10] *Statist*, February 22, 1902, p. 407.

[11] F. Schuster, "Foreign Trade and the Money Market," *Journal of the Institute of Bankers*, February 1904, p. 61.

[12] *Op.cit.*, p. 125. See also Morgan, *Studies in British Financial Policy*, p. 332; and F. W. Paish, "The United Kingdom as a Source of Capital," *District Bank Review*, March 1953, p. 4. In an earlier study, Morgan had stated that before the third quarter of the 19th century England had been a net short-term *debtor*. See E. V. Morgan, *The Theory and Practice of Central Banking, 1797-1913* (Cambridge, England, 1943), pp. 170, 217, 225.

[13] *Op.cit.*, pp. 149, 150.

[14] J. M. Keynes, *A Treatise on Money* (London, 1930), Vol. II, p. 316.

may have alternately shifted from a net short-term creditor to debtor position, and vice versa, under the impact of cyclical fluctuations in interest-rate differentials between London and foreign centers, swings in Britain's balance of payments on current and long-term capital account, and a variety of other factors.

There has long been recognition of the fact that before 1914 increases in the Bank of England discount rate, when "effective" in the market and not offset by corresponding increases in other leading centers, had an important short-run effect in stemming drains on the gold reserves of the Bank of England (whether external or internal in origin), and even in reversing the flow of gold, by inducing equilibrating inflows of capital.[15] Higher interest rates discouraged foreign short-term borrowings in London, thereby resulting, given the amount of its foreign short-term claims regularly falling due, in a net excess of repayments. Foreign short-term funds were also attracted into sterling bills and other money-market assets, and foreigners were encouraged to retain sterling balances they might have otherwise repatriated or transferred elsewhere. In addition, Britishers were induced to repatriate funds invested at short-term in foreign money markets. Finally, the flotation of foreign securities in the London market tended to be temporarily postponed. To the extent that the higher interest rates in London were associated with a fall in the pound to its gold export point, i.e., with an external gold drain, these equilibrating shifts in the flow of capital would tend to be reinforced.

On all this there has been broad agreement. But various authorities have gone further by making assertions as to the relative quantitative importance of the reaction to discount-rate increases of the major components of the short-term capital flow. The more common view is that Britain's short-term foreign assets contracted by more than its short-term liabilities rose. The Macmillan Report expressed this view as follows: "A rise in discount rates in the pre-war money market functioned mainly by calling in our claims on the rest of the world through the contraction in the volume of our acceptances."[16] Similarly, Schumpeter stated that England's short-term foreign claims "responded to the Bank's slightest move very much more promptly than foreign-owned

[15] There has been much less agreement as to the effectiveness and precise *modus operandi* of the longer-run effects of an increase in Bank Rate. For a well-balanced recent discussion, see A. G. Ford, *The Gold Standard, 1880-1914: Britain and Argentina* (Oxford, 1962), pp. 30-48.

[16] *Op.cit.*, p. 149.

balances would have done."[17] Harrod, in fact, almost seems to question whether a rise in the Bank's discount rate had any effect upon foreign short-term funds at all.[18] As opposed to this point of view, however, the Cunliffe Report of 1918 discussed the short-run effects of a discount-rate increase without any explicit reference to Britain's foreign short-term claims. A rise in the Bank rate, it stated, "had the immediate effect of retaining money here which would otherwise have been remitted abroad and of attracting remittances from abroad to take advantage of the higher rate."[19]

Firm generalizations on this matter, one way or the other, would seem, however, to be suspect. The more common view that England's foreign short-term claims tended to react more sharply in absolute terms to discount-rate increases than did its liabilities seems to rest upon the assumptions that the outstanding volume of the former was at any time usually substantially in excess of the latter, and that it was somehow *easier*—in a way never clearly explained—for a country in Britain's position to contract its short-term foreign credits than to increase its foreign liabilities.[20] But what really mattered was not the relative sizes of each at any given time, but the degree of sensitivity of each to discount-rate increases; and the latter need have borne no necessary relationship to the former.

On the assets side, for example, one would have to draw a distinction between acceptances representing commercial bills and finance bills, respectively. The former, it is generally believed, do not appear to have been much affected by higher short-term interest rates in London. Foreign importers in the pre-1914 world were not able easily to shift acceptance financing to other centers, simply because the necessary facilities outside of London were generally quite limited.[21] Besides, foreign commercial borrowers were in any case probably reluctant to alter long-standing credit lines or banking connections in London because of temporary rate increases and to shop around for alternative sources of

[17] Schumpeter, *Business Cycles*, Vol. II, p. 673.

[18] Thus he states that an adverse British balance of payments before 1914 "was corrected by a rise in short-term interest rates discouraging foreign borrowers and *perhaps even* attracting short-term funds from abroad" [italics mine]. See R. F. Harrod, *Policy Against Inflation* (New York, 1958), pp. 14-15.

[19] See *First Interim Report: Committee on Currency and Foreign Exchanges*, 1918, reprinted in T. E. Gregory, *Selected Statutes and Documents* (Oxford, 1929), p. 336.

[20] See, e.g., Keynes, *Indian Currency and Finance*, p. 18.

[21] To some extent, however, foreign importers might have shifted from acceptance financing in London to borrowings from banks elsewhere.

credit elsewhere. It is not likely, moreover, that a rise in the discount rate as such would have made London accepting houses, whose main concern was the ratio of their acceptance liabilities to their capital, less willing to enter into acceptance commitments on behalf of credit-worthy foreign customers. London discount houses, however, at a time of monetary stringency, might have been somewhat more reluctant to take up bills that were offered or have been more selective in their pur-chases. On the other hand, foreign drawings of *finance* bills on London houses appear to have been quite sensitive to higher short-term interest rates, since these borrowings were motivated primarily by relative interest rates in London and abroad.[22] To the extent that a rise in the Bank rate had the effect of reducing Britain's foreign acceptance claims, it was mainly on this component, which may have represented more than half of the outstanding total in 1913, that it must have acted.

Even less can be said with regard to the liabilities side. One simply does not know how large a volume of foreign short-term funds was char-acteristically attracted from abroad under the impact of a given dis-count-rate increase. Nor can one make any reasoned statements as to the amount of foreign-owned balances in England that would have normally been withdrawn but was instead temporarily retained be-cause of the given rate increase. Even if Britain's outstanding short-term foreign claims *did* usually exceed its short-term foreign liabilities, there seems to be no necessary reason why the former should have tended to contract by more than the latter increased—or indeed conversely—as the discount rate rose. Only the availability of the relevant statistics would help to provide the answer.

Lack of statistical data regarding Britain's foreign short-term claims likewise makes it impossible to test the validity of one aspect of the widely held view that London "managed" the international gold-stand-ard system before 1914 and that its wise management contributed materially to the successful functioning of that system. There can be no doubt that the Bank of England managed *Britain's* own gold stand-ard, for the most part successfully, but whether or not the Bank or the City of London managed the international gold standard in some broader sense on behalf of the various participants is another question. Management in this wider sense has been interpreted in a variety of ways, not always clearly expressed, and could have taken a variety of

[22] See, e.g., Brown, *International Gold Standard Reinterpreted*, Vol. I, pp. 652-653 and 665-666; and Kindersley in *Minutes of Evidence*, Vol. I, p. 76.

possible forms. Only one of these is directly relevant here. As Viner states it:

> London, by granting [short-term] credit abroad more freely in times of strain and contracting it in times of dangerous expansion, could have exercised a stabilizing rôle *vis-à-vis* the international gold standard. . . . But I know of no evidence that London played such a rôle, and as far as available information goes it may even be possible that London typically reduced her credits to abroad when it was most urgent that she should expand them and expanded them when contraction would have been more beneficial.[23]

One observation that can be made quite safely is that, if London *did* "manage" the international gold standard in this sense, it did not do so deliberately, as the concept of management would imply. London financial institutions were overwhelmingly concerned with their liquidity and solvency and the profitability of their operations, and did not consciously adjust the volume of their foreign short-term credits in general—if indeed they themselves took the initiative in doing so—unless it was in their own interests. But whether or not these credits did in fact vary in accord with the requirements of international financial stability, or on the contrary, as Viner suggests, followed a "perverse" pattern, cannot be definitively answered in the absence of statistics of Britain's short-term foreign credits.

## Other Countries

Although Germany was for many years before 1914 a large net creditor on long-term international account, there is an almost complete lack of information regarding the status of her net short-term foreign position. On both the assets and liabilities sides, statistical data are virtually nonexistent.

It is well known that German banks, especially after 1900, borrowed

---

[23] J. Viner, "Clapham on the Bank of England," *Economica*, May 1945, pp. 63-64. For a statement of the more traditional view in this respect, see E. S. Shaw, *Money, Income, and Monetary Policy* (Chicago, 1950), p. 567: "Great Britain was the pre-1914 International Monetary Fund. Her loans to countries having temporary difficulties with their balances of payments saved the borrowers from gold exports, exchange depreciation, or internal deflation." For an extreme statement, see J. H. Jones, "The Gold Standard," *Economic Journal*, December 1933, p. 564: "One of the outstanding features of the system was that, when any country was in distress, the Bank of England was able and ready to mobilize the resources of the world and rush to the rescue of that country."

heavily at short-term abroad, mainly in Paris and London where short-term interest rates were generally lower, but also in New York, Amsterdam, Brussels, and Zurich. These borrowings took the form primarily of pensioning of mark bills and drawing of finance bills on the centers concerned. As an important international financial center engaged in long-term foreign lending and trade financing, Berlin also had large deposit liabilities to foreigners and associated short-term foreign obligations.[24] It has been estimated that Germany's foreign short-term debt on banking account just before the war may have amounted to about one billion marks ($238 million) and that it had increased by approximately 50 per cent since 1900.[25] This estimate, which is no more than an intelligent guess, presumably does not include Germany's debts on purely commercial account, as well as the outstanding amounts of short-term issues that had been placed abroad by the German Government and its subdivisions.

On the other side of the balance sheet, Germany had substantial short-term claims on foreign countries. These included banking credits, mainly to Russia and other Eastern European countries, holdings of foreign bills and other balances abroad, and undoubtedly very large trade credits. Except for the foreign balances of the Reichsbank, however, amounting to over 200 million marks in 1913, statistical information is extremely limited. Only a few of the German banks reported their holdings of foreign bills and other foreign claims, and then only for isolated dates.[26]

On balance, Germany's usual short-term foreign position in the years just before 1914 is generally believed to have been that of a net debtor, but it could well have been the other way around. It may be significant that Keynes, writing in 1913, stated merely that in the international short-term loan market Germany was a creditor in relation to some of her neighbors but likely to be a debtor in relation to France, Great Britain, and the United States.[27] On the other hand, he was quite explicit in stating that Britain and France were net short-term foreign creditors. Some authorities, moreover, felt that the extent of Germany's

[24] See, e.g., W. Mueller, "The Organization of Credit and Banking Arrangements in Germany," *Miscellaneous Articles on German Banking*, National Monetary Commission (Washington, 1910), pp. 143-144; and R. Franz, "The Statistical History of the German Banking System," *ibid.*, pp. 73-74.

[25] J. T. Madden and M. Nadler, *The International Money Markets* (New York, 1935), p. 362; and Neisser, *Weltwirtschaftliches Archiv*, April 1929, p. 206. (Neisser's estimate, which is the same as Madden's and Nadler's, is actually for late 1911.)

[26] For some examples, see Reisser, *German Great Banks*, p. 262.

[27] *Indian Currency and Finance*, p. 27.

78

short-term foreign debts had been exaggerated and its short-term foreign claims underestimated.[28] Of possible relevance in this connection is the fact that in its annual report for 1911 the Deutsche Bank—the largest German bank—reported that for years its short-term foreign liabilities had always been balanced by its short-term assets abroad and at times had actually been exceeded by them.[29]

Statistical information regarding the short-term foreign position of the United States before 1914 is not much better. Reference has already been made to the importance of American borrowings in Europe on finance bills, the outstanding total of which at their peak in 1906 was estimated by Sprague at some $400-500 million. In 1911 Paish estimated that outstanding American borrowings in Europe on finance bills, produce bills, loans against securities, overdrafts, etc., while fluctuating seasonally, averaged about $400 million over the course of the year.[30] Another writer has estimated that *aggregate* United States short-term foreign liabilities rose from $250 million at the end of 1897 to $400 million at the end of 1908 and to $450 million by July 1914.[31] These totals, however, are not broken down into their components; and one wonders whether adequate allowance has been made for liabilities other than bank borrowings, including foreign funds in the New York call market and foreign holdings of commercial paper and bank deposits, the aggregate of which at times must have reached very significant dimensions. Canadian banks alone, according to the series described earlier, had call and short loans in the United States of $97 million at the end of 1908 and $125 million in July 1914, as well as short-term claims on American banks of $35 million and $44 million on these two dates, respectively.

Estimates of American short-term assets abroad are completely lacking. These assets undoubtedly grew rapidly after 1900 with the expanding role of the United States in international finance. Apart from an evidently substantial growth in American deposits abroad and holdings of foreign bills,[32] the United States appears increasingly to have

[28] For a brief survey of some German discussions on this matter, see K. Bopp, "Die Tätigkeit der Reichsbank von 1876 bis 1914," *Weltwirtschaftliches Archiv* (1954 II), pp. 212-213.

[29] Cited in J. Plenge, *Von der Diskontpolitik zur Herrschaft über den Geldmarkt* (Berlin, 1913), p. 265.

[30] Sir George Paish, "The Trade Balance of the United States," in *Miscellaneous Articles*, National Monetary Commission (Washington, 1911), p. 175.

[31] C. Lewis, *America's Stake in International Investments* (Washington, 1938), pp. 442, 445.

[32] For example, a foreign-exchange expert referred in 1913 to the fact that the

become a short-term lender to foreign banks and governments.[33] On balance, however, it is probable that just before the war the United States was a net short-term foreign debtor, but a considerably smaller one than it had been a decade earlier. It was, of course, a large net debtor on long-term account.

With regard to Russia, statistics of the short-term foreign borrowings and assets of the commercial banks are available for the six years before 1914. These statistics, along with those of official Russian balances abroad which were examined earlier in this study, are brought together in Table III.

The table indicates that while the Russian commercial banks had a large net short-term debtor position with foreign countries—in substantial part because of borrowings from French and German banks—this was more than offset by Russian official holdings of foreign exchange.

TABLE III

Russian Short-term Foreign Assets and Liabilities

(millions of rubles)

| Year (Jan. 1) | Foreign Short-term Credits to Russian Commercial Banks[a] | Foreign Short-term Assets of Russian Commercial Banks[a] | Official Russian Balances Abroad[b] | Net Short-term Creditor Position |
|---|---|---|---|---|
| 1909 | 240 | 57 | 200 | 17 ($8.8 million) |
| 1910 | 209 | 18 | 517 | 326 ($169.5 " ) |
| 1911 | 268 | 81 | 579 | 392 ($203.8 " ) |
| 1912 | 446 | 168 | 587 | 309 ($160.7 " ) |
| 1913 | 500 | 190 | 652 | 342 ($176.1 " ) |
| 1914 | 546 | 207 | 594 | 255 ($132.6 " ) |

[a] I. F. Gindin, *Russkiye Kommercheskiye Banki* (Moscow, 1948), p. 254. I am indebted to Dr. Olga Crisp for calling my attention to this book and to my colleague, Dr. Herbert S. Levine, for translating relevant passages for me.

[b] See Appendix III below.

---

number of American banks all over the country that kept deposit accounts in leading European countries had become "surprisingly great" during the preceding decade. See F. Escher, *Elements of Foreign Exchange*, Third Edition (New York, 1913), p. 425.

[33] For example, American short-term credits to Germany alone were estimated at between $60-70 million in October 1911 by the *Economist*, October 28, 1911, p. 862. United States investors are also reported to have taken up issues of Prussian and Austrian Treasury bills and other foreign short-term foreign issues. See *Economist*, November 4, 1911, p. 922, and *ibid.*, December 14, 1912, pp. 1205-1206.

To what extent the resulting net creditor position might in turn have been counterbalanced by the short-term foreign borrowings of Russian commercial concerns and of the Russian Government itself is not known. On *long-term* account, however, Russia had the largest foreign liabilities of any country in the world.

Italy was another large short-term borrower abroad before 1914. According to one estimate, the outstanding short-term foreign debt of that country on banking and commercial account at the end of 1914 had grown to at least 500 million lire ($95 million).[34] Another writer has estimated that between 1900-1913 short-term foreign claims on Italy rose by 300 million lire,[35] which suggests that Italy's short-term foreign debt in 1900 may have been about 200 million lire. According to the same writer, Italian short-term assets abroad *also* rose by about 300 million between 1900-1913, so that Italy's *net* short-term foreign position during that period remained roughly unchanged. A small part of that increase (about 35 million lire) reflected the net growth in the foreign balances of the three issue banks and the Italian Treasury discussed earlier in this study. While no estimates are available for the country's aggregate outstanding foreign short-term claims, it is probable that on balance Italy was a net short-term foreign debtor at the outbreak of the war. On long-term account the country remained a net debtor, although its position in this respect had improved considerably in the decade before 1914 with the rapid repatriation of its public debt held abroad.

Statistical information is even more fragmentary for other European gold-standard countries. Switzerland, Holland, and Belgium were all net long-term creditors, but virtually nothing is known, apart from official holdings of balances abroad, as to the size of their short-term claims and liabilities. With regard to Austria-Hungary even the published statistics of official foreign balances are known to be incomplete.[36]

As for Switzerland, annual data are available for the combined foreign-bill holdings of the commercial banks and central bank from

[34] C. E. McGuire, *Italy's International Economic Position* (New York, 1926), p. 287.

[35] E. Corbino, *Annali dell'Economia Italiana*, Vol. V, 1901-1914 (Città di Castello, 1938), p. 222.

[36] Annual data are available, however, for the *Devisen* (foreign-exchange) holdings of the *Austrian* commercial banks from 1903-1913 in various issues of the Austrian *Statistisches Jahrbuch*. It is not known how comprehensive these statistics are supposed to be. At the end of 1913 the total amounted to 60.4 million crown (roughly $12 million), and during the period ranged from 42.5 to 106.6 million crown.

1906-1913, the total amounting at the end of 1913 to 76.3 million francs ($14.5 million) and ranging during the period from 62.9 to 112.7 million francs.[37] There are no statistics for other Swiss assets or liabilities. Switzerland is known to have held substantial short-term foreign claims in the form of loans on foreign money markets and to have occasionally borrowed in Paris by pensioning Swiss bills.[38] There is also reason to believe that floating foreign funds found their way in volume into Swiss banks.

Although the exact size and status of the net short-term creditor-debtor position of a given country are not, as that term has been defined here, of major significance as such, the foregoing survey of the net short-term positions of some of the leading gold-standard countries has provided a convenient framework for bringing together such statistical data and estimates as are available regarding the volume and constituent components of the foreign short-term assets and liabilities of these countries in the years just before World War I. In only a few of these cases has it been possible to establish what the net positions of the individual countries characteristically were in view of the limitations of the available information. Nevertheless, it would appear that net foreign positions on short-term account were usually very small in relation to the corresponding positions on long-term account, that they fluctuated much more sharply than the latter from year to year, and that in some cases they may have even shifted from net creditor to net debtor status and vice versa within relatively short periods of time.

[37] See "Das schweizerische Bankwesen in den Jahren 1906-1913," *Zeitschrift für schweizerische Statistik*, 1915, p. 561. An annual series dating back to 1871 is also available for the foreign-bill holdings of the approximately 30 Swiss note-issuing banks before the establishment of the National Bank in 1907. See A. Johr, *Die schweizerischen Notenbanken, 1826-1913* (Zurich, 1915), Vol. II, p. 454. But these banks covered less than half of the resources of the Swiss banking system.

[38] For some details as to the nature of Swiss short-term assets and liabilities just before 1914, see W. Zollinger, *Die Bilanz der internationalen Wertübertragungen* (Jena, 1914), pp. 159-161.

# V. ABNORMAL MOVEMENTS OF SHORT-TERM CAPITAL

It is frequently stated that capital flight, capital flows associated with destabilizing exchange speculation, and other forms of "abnormal" movements of short-term capital were of trifling importance under the pre-1914 gold standard. Certainly such movements were of relatively much less importance then than they were thereafter. But they were far from being virtually non-existent, as some of the more extreme assertions would have it.[1] On the contrary, an examination of the period suggests that "hot-money" flows were more common than seems to be generally believed.

Abnormal capital movements will be broadly defined here to include (a) movements associated with destabilizing exchange speculation, and (b) movements motivated by a desire to avoid the risk of loss or impairment of capital because of actual or anticipated wars, internal political upheavals, collapse of the banking system, high taxation, or other such disturbances or factors (capital flight proper). Such movements may involve short-term or long-term assets, private or official funds, and, from the viewpoint of any given country, exports or imports of domestic or foreign capital. They usually, but by no means invariably, tend to flow from high- to low-interest-rate countries and from countries with payments deficits and/or to countries with payments surpluses. The focus here will be mainly on those abnormal capital movements that involved private short-term funds.

For those countries which were not members of the gold-standard group and whose exchange rates fluctuated in terms of gold—countries which are largely excluded from the scope of this study—destabilizing exchange speculation must at times have assumed great importance in accentuating the degree of exchange-rate fluctuations. This at once suggests itself on the basis of even a cursory examination of the disordered monetary histories of such countries as Spain, Greece, and

[1] See, e.g., B. Ohlin, *International Economic Reconstruction* (Paris, 1936), p. 34: "During a pre-war period of relatively peaceful sentiments and no important and lasting wars, floating balances of this . . . disturbing sort practically did not exist." See also J. A. Stovel, *Canada in the World Economy* (Cambridge, Mass., 1959), p. 60: "The volatile shifts of autonomous short-term capital which attracted so much attention in the interwar period were . . . notably absent prior to 1914." Likewise, see Shaw, *Money, Income, and Monetary Policy*, p. 566: ". . . there was [before 1914] no fund of flight capital to drive gold from market to market, because of the prevailing confidence in the stability of exchange rates."

the great majority of Latin American countries before 1914, or of Russia, Austria-Hungary, Italy, and Japan before they linked up with gold around 1900.

But even the stability of certain gold currencies was not always implicitly accepted. We are referring here not to the expectation of slight declines in the exchange rates concerned beyond their accustomed limits because of fractional increases in the selling price of gold or related official actions, but to the anticipation of the more significant declines that would be associated with a lapse into floating rates ("inconvertibility") or formal exchange devaluation. Two important cases may be cited where such anticipations prevailed and appear to have induced large capital outflows.

In 1905-1906 Russia came close to abandoning the gold standard because of heavy drains on its gold and foreign-exchange reserves which were accentuated by capital flight and destabilizing speculation against the ruble. The financing of the disastrous Russo-Japanese war of 1904-1905 had led to rapid currency inflation and to big deficits in the balance of payments. The war and the revolution which followed it provoked a large-scale flight of capital to France and other foreign countries. Expectations of an abandonment of gold led to, and were further strengthened by, heavy speculative purchases of foreign exchange (in the forward as well as the spot market), withdrawals of foreign balances in Russia, and runs on the banks for payment in gold only. In the face of the rapidly deteriorating situation, the State Bank imposed temporarily a limited form of exchange control[2] and took steps to restrain internal demands for gold. The Russian Government even went so far as to draft a law suspending the gold standard.[3] Confidence appears to have been restored mainly by the grant to the government in April 1906 of a loan of over 2 billion francs by a consortium of French, British, and other European private banks.[4] Thereafter Russia's position steadily improved. But fears of further internal political upheavals continued to provoke creeping flights of capital by the wealthy classes.

The American dollar was subject to intermittent speculative attacks during the 1890's, especially from 1893 to 1896 when there were periodic doubts at home and abroad as to the ability of the United States to maintain the gold standard. Under the impact of the world

[2] Slansky, *La Banque Impériale de Russie*, pp. 94-95.
[3] Bernatzky in *Russian Public Finance During the War*, pp. 348-350.
[4] O. Crisp, "The Russian Liberals and the 1906 Anglo-French Loan to Russia," *The Slavonic and East European Review*, June 1961, pp. 497-500.

depression, the panic of 1893, Treasury fiscal difficulties, the passage of the Sherman Silver Act of 1890 (repealed in 1893), and the increasing bimetallist agitation which reached a peak during the Presidential election campaign of 1896, there were intermittently heavy liquidations by foreigners of dollar balances and American securities, speculative purchases by Americans of foreign exchange, and unusually large internal drains of gold—all of which put the Treasury's gold stock under severe pressure and further strengthened the incentive for speculative capital outflows and gold withdrawals. The Treasury, in order to protect its dwindling gold reserve, was forced into a series of expedients, including sales of bonds for gold at home and abroad, and purchases of gold from the banks for legal-tender currency. In addition, a syndicate of American bankers cooperated by introducing in 1895 a system of "private exchange control," and by forming in 1896 a private "pool" of foreign exchange, constituted from short-term credits obtained abroad, which was used to keep the dollar above its gold export point.[5] It was only after the defeat in 1896 of the Democratic Party, with its "free-silver" program, that the threat to the gold standard in the United States came to an end.[6]

Although concrete evidence is lacking, it is quite possible that certain other gold currencies may at times have been subject to speculative attacks arising from a belief that parity could not be maintained. We know, for example, that on a number of occasions the reserve position of certain gold-standard countries deteriorated so seriously that "extraordinary" measures had to be taken to protect convertibility. It would seem reasonable to assume that on such occasions there must have been some speculative selling of the currencies concerned.

While the period 1880-1914 was free of global armed conflicts, it witnessed a substantial number of localized wars,[7] and increasing international political tensions and crises that culminated in World War I. These developments, if one is to judge from comments in the contemporary financial press and other sources, prompted capital flights and other politically motivated movements of short-term funds that at times

[5] For a detailed account of the latter episode, see M. Simon, "The Hot Money Movement and the Private Exchange Pool Proposal of 1896," *Journal of Economic History*, March 1960, pp. 31-50.

[6] For a narrative of this whole period, see Noyes, *Forty Years of American Finance*, pp. 152-256.

[7] In addition to the Russo-Japanese War, one might cite the Sino-Japanese War (1894-1895), the Spanish-American War (1898), the Boer War (1899-1902), the Italian-Turkish War (1911-1912), and the two Balkan Wars (1912-1913).

must have reached significant proportions by pre-1914 standards. One of the more notable examples is provided by the heavy withdrawals of French short-term credits and balances in Germany from July to October 1911, when Franco-German tension over Morocco, which had been simmering for years, reached its peak with the Agadir crisis.[8] Although estimates of the sums withdrawn during this period have varied widely, the *Economist* placed the total, including smaller amounts withdrawn by other European countries, at about £40 million ($195 million).[9] The gold and exchange reserves of the Reichsbank were drawn down sharply and the Berlin money market put under heavy strain. Deteriorating political relations among European countries in general, and shadows of the approaching global war, undoubtedly exerted an increasingly disturbing influence upon movements of short-term funds in the years immediately before 1914.

Consider now briefly an example of abnormal short-term capital movements where the motive was fear of a collapse of the banking system. During the great Australian land boom of the 1880's and early 1890's, British investors, apart from their purchases of Australian securities, had placed large amounts of fixed deposits with banks in that country in view of the attractive rates of interest paid and the aggressive solicitation of such deposits in England and Scotland by agents of these banks.[10] By the end of 1891 the total of these deposits, most of which matured in one year, had reached a peak of almost £40 million.[11] By 1890 concern was already growing as to the overextended foreign debt of Australia and the precarious foundations of its prosperity. The failure of a large number of building societies and land companies in 1891-1892 brought down several banks and led to growing fears as to the position of the banking system as a whole. By May 1893, when the panic was in full swing, three of the banks were in liquidation and 13 others had suspended payments.[12]

[8] See, e.g., J. Lescure, "Les Marchés Financiers de Berlin et de Paris et la Crise Franco-Allemande de Juillet-Octobre 1911," *Revue Economique Internationale*, September 1912, pp. 466-509.

[9] *Economist*, October 21, 1911, p. 813. The French Government, in order to exert pressure on Germany, undoubtedly played an important part in provoking the withdrawals by the French banks. See E. A. Staley, *War and the Private Investor* (Chicago, 1935), p. 94.

[10] The deposits were repayable in pounds sterling, not Australian pounds.

[11] T. A. Coughlan, *Labor and Industry in Australia* (Oxford, 1918), Vol. III, p. 1640. On the same date some £10 million of British fixed deposits, most with maturities of more than one year, were also held in Australian building societies, finance companies, and trading companies.

[12] A. S. J. Baster, *The Imperial Banks* (London, 1929), p. 149.

During the emerging banking crisis, British depositors withdrew their deposits as they matured, when this was still possible. But these withdrawals were not the major cause of the bank failures and suspensions of payments. The run on the banks was mainly undertaken by Australian depositors, since British deposits could be withdrawn only on maturity. It was rather the fear by the banks of large withdrawals of these deposits as they matured that played a causal role of great importance in the banking crisis.[13] With the resumption of payments and the reorganization of some of the banks after the panic, British deposits continued to be withdrawn and by the end of 1900 had declined to £13.5 million.[14]

Capital movements motivated by a desire to evade or avoid taxes could hardly have been of much consequence before 1914 in view of the low burden of direct taxes that prevailed. Yet even this kind of capital flight was at times in evidence. For example, in the spring of 1913 it was reported that the amount of German funds moving to Switzerland because of fears of heavy taxation in Germany was increasing rapidly.[15] And it has been noted that low taxes were one of the factors that made Belgium a refuge for foreign, and especially French, capital.[16]

The isolated examples given above, the list of which could easily be extended, indicate that abnormal short-term capital movements in their various forms were by no means unknown between gold-standard countries before 1914. The evidence, indeed, suggests that these movements, particularly of the capital-flight variety, were more common and may at times have been more disturbing in their balance-of-payments effects than is customarily assumed. On the other hand, when viewed in the light of the magnitude, disruptive force, and highly erratic character of the hot-money flows of the post-1914 period, they admittedly pale into relative insignificance.

Quite apart from the problem of abnormal capital flows, individual

13 Coughlan, op.cit., Vol. III, pp. 1654-1656.

14 During the New Zealand banking crisis of 1894-1895, there were similar withdrawals of British fixed deposits that had been built up in the banks of that country. See C. F. G. Simkin, The Instability of a Dependent Economy (Oxford, 1951), pp. 79, 153-154. Pre-1914 American experience would undoubtedly provide examples of this kind of capital flight because of the weakness of the commercial banking system and its suspension of cash payments during the three great crises of the 19th and early 20th centuries.

15 Economist, April 19, 1913, pp. 935-936.

16 B. S. Chlepner, Le Marché Financier Belge Depuis Cent Ans (Brussels, 1930), p. 87.

countries were frequently subjected to large and sudden outflows of short-term funds that were of a "normal" character but disequilibrating in their effects on the balance of payments. For example, as noted earlier, a sharp rise in short-term interest rates in a leading financial center could induce large outflows of foreign (and domestic) funds from other countries that might cause or accentuate drains on their official reserves. Most serious were the outflows induced by liquidity crises abroad at times of financial panics (e.g., 1900, 1907), when banks and other parties in the centers immediately concerned tended to call in their foreign credits and withdraw their foreign balances in order to help strengthen their liquidity positions. Other factors contributed to sudden repatriations of foreign short-term funds from given countries or to their transfer to other centers. For example, French banks are reported on occasion to have withdrawn some of their balances abroad in order to strengthen their resources in view of large pending foreign flotations on the Paris market.[17] The pre-1914 period is replete with examples of such disturbing movements of funds resulting from these and other causes. In addition, as has been noted earlier, foreign-owned *official* balances appear at times to have been shifted from center to center in a capricious manner.

Recognition of the potential dangers inherent in a large short-term foreign indebtedness was of course by no means new. But after 1900, with the increase in the volume and volatility of international short-term capital movements, there were more frequent expressions of concern in various countries, especially in Great Britain[18] and Germany,[19] as to their vulnerability to sudden outflows of funds under the impact of financial and political developments abroad that could subject them to disturbingly large gold drains and unsettling money-market effects.

[17] *Economist*, October 29, 1904, p. 1725; January 14, 1905, p. 38; and February 18, 1905 (supplement), pp. 4-5.

[18] See, e.g., "Colonial and Foreign Banks in England and the Banking Reserve," *The Bankers Magazine*, March 1900; W. R. Lawson, "Lombard Street Under Foreign Control," *ibid.*, March 1901; and "The Bank of England and the Money Market," *ibid.*, March 1906. The *Statist* (February 22, 1902, p. 408), after referring to the fact that foreign short-term money in London was then "much in excess of anything before known," called attention to the danger that it involved if interest rates on the continent fell much below London or if for any reason continental banks found it necessary to strengthen their positions at home.

[19] See, e.g., the interesting remarks of A. Schmidt in *German Banking Inquiry of 1908-9*, National Monetary Commission (Washington, 1911), pp. 292-293 and 645-646, and especially his statement (p. 293) that foreign balances, because of their special susceptibility to withdrawal, "demand much greater attention . . . than the credit balances of the regular and permanent customers at home."

To be sure, discount-rate increases and related policy measures had, at least in Britain and certain of the other leading gold-standard countries, generally demonstrated their effectiveness in stemming gold losses, but there was no assurance that they would always suffice to protect convertibility. In the case of the smaller gold countries, such instruments would in any case have been of little avail. In Britain and Germany the existence of large foreign short-term balances liable to sudden withdrawal gave added impetus to the growing agitation for larger gold reserves in the years just before 1914.

# VI. CONCLUDING NOTE

This study has brought together and analyzed a variety of statistical data and other materials relating to the nature, pattern, and role of short-term capital movements from 1880 to 1914 in an effort to throw some additional empirical light on an important element in the functioning of the pre-1914 gold-standard system. It does not pretend to cover all aspects of its subject-matter. Nothing has been said here, for example, about the internal money-market effects of such movements; and only incidental attention has been paid to the various techniques other than discount-rate policy, such as manipulations of the gold points, official intervention in the forward-exchange market, and the like, whereby monetary authorities from time to time attempted to influence the flow of private short-term funds in desired directions.[1] Nor has any effort been made to deal with those aspects of the subject already treated in some detail elsewhere, notably in the painstaking statistical studies of Morgenstern and Neisser.

The materials assembled here, despite their limitations and the serious deficiencies in particular of the statistical data on private short-term capital movements, cast some doubt upon the validity of some of the simple generalizations that have all too frequently been made in this area. Movements of private short-term funds were more complex in nature and motivation than is customarily assumed in standard treatments of the pre-1914 system. Unquestionably, short-term interest-rate differentials and exchange-rate fluctuations within the gold points played a dominant role in directing the flow of private short-term funds between gold-standard countries, even if the degree of mobility of the funds so motivated has sometimes been exaggerated. But by no means all private short-term capital movements can be explained in these simple terms. Preferences, based on institutional arrangements or long-standing banking connections, as to foreign lenders or as to markets in which to place short-term funds; the availability of credit as contrasted with its cost; the requirements of external debt service; the changing needs for maintaining working balances in given centers; considerations of bank liquidity: all these and other factors exerted an influence on the volume and direction of short-term capital flows that may at times have overshadowed interest-rate and exchange-rate fac-

[1] These techniques were outlined in somewhat more detail in my earlier study.

tors. Capital flights and other "abnormal" movements of liquid funds were, moreover, of greater importance than is usually believed. And even when of a "normal" character, private short-term capital movements were by no means always equilibrating in their balance-of-payments effects.

Threats to convertibility, at times induced or accentuated by disequilibrating capital outflows, on more than one occasion necessitated "extraordinary" defensive measures going well beyond discount-rate increases, which were in any case a rather weak reed for most gold-standard countries to lean upon even in normal times. For example, in a number of instances monetary authorities were forced to arrange emergency borrowings of gold and foreign credits in order to cope with dangerous drains on their reserves, and in at least two cases (the United States and Russia) resort was had temporarily to limited forms of exchange control.

The outstanding volume of international short-term balances appears to have grown substantially in size over the period, especially after 1900. This is clearly confirmed, at least so far as official balances were concerned, by our statistical series on official foreign-exchange holdings, the upward trend of which reflected the spread and development of gold-exchange-standard arrangements.[2] Judging from our other statistical data—much more limited though they are—and especially from contemporary comment in the financial press and elsewhere, there was likewise a marked increase in the outstanding volume of private short-term foreign balances and claims. With this over-all growth, and the increased volatility of short-term capital that appears to have accompanied it, increasing concern was expressed in a number of countries as to the danger of sudden withdrawals of foreign funds and short-term credits and as to the appropriateness of the level of their reserves available to meet such withdrawals and other payments strains. After 1907, moreover, there was a growing sentiment in certain quarters in favor of some kind of systematic international monetary cooperation, the absence of which was a conspicuous feature of the pre-1914 arrangements, in order to minimize undue shocks to the payments system from these and other sources.

With its emphasis on short-term capital movements, this study has of course focused only on the short-term adjustment processes of the pre-1914 gold standard. It has not dealt with the "longer-run" or more fundamental forces working to correct any persisting payments dis-

---

[2] As we have seen, however, official gold holdings rose by much more.

equilibria and which, whatever their exact form, contributed to the successful maintenance of the international gold standard. From the short-term point of view, when all is said and done, private short-term capital movements, despite their often erratic, perverse, and disequilibrating character, unquestionably played a role of key importance in tiding countries over periods of temporary payments imbalances and in cushioning their effects upon official reserves. The statistical data for the four Scandinavian countries, incidentally, lend a measure of support to the view that these movements were in the main equilibrating in character. And while official foreign-owned balances were at times capriciously shifted from center to center or converted into gold, official short-term capital movements themselves appear to have predominantly played an "accommodating" role in international balances of payments.

From what little statistical evidence we have, it would seem that the international short-term creditor-debtor positions of individual countries tended to fluctuate substantially within relatively short periods of time. Indeed, with gross short-term foreign assets for many countries probably not differing greatly from their gross short-term foreign liabilities, frequent shifts from net creditor to net debtor positions on short-term account, and vice versa, were undoubtedly not unusual. At any time, moreover, a country's net short-term position was likely to have been only relatively small compared with its net foreign position on long-term account.

Our limited sample of statistical series on private short-term capital movements throws little light on the question of whether or not such movements tended to exhibit any consistent pattern in relation to business cycles. In the case of Finland, Denmark, and Sweden, the net foreign assets of the commercial banks tended to conform inversely to domestic business fluctuations, but no conformity was indicated in the French or Norwegian series. On theoretical grounds there is in any case no necessary reason for expecting any consistent pattern in this respect as among individual countries. Absence of the necessary statistical data made impossible a direct testing of the well-known thesis of Beach[3] that in the case of Great Britain and the United States short-term capital movements tended on balance to be inwards during periods of domestic prosperity and outwards during recessions.

While there can of course be no question as to the preeminence of

[3] W. E. Beach, *British International Gold Movements and Banking Policy, 1881-1913* (Cambridge, Mass., 1935).

Great Britain as an international reserve center and short-term foreign lender under the pre-1914 system, the statistical information and other materials presented here suggest that the uniqueness of Britain's position in the international money market may have often been somewhat exaggerated. As we have seen, large foreign balances were also held in France and Germany, and both of these countries, especially the former, were important short-term international lenders. Even the growing role of the United States in these respects in the later years of the period may have been underestimated. In any case, stereotyped assertions to the effect that before 1914 the world outside Great Britain "was on a sterling-exchange standard"—managed by the City of London in the interests of the stability of the gold-standard system as a whole—are evident over-simplifications.

Twenty-five years ago Viner wrote that "international short-term lending still awaits its historian."[4] Among other things, the present study has brought together, for the limited but important period covered here, many of the basic materials for such a history. But the serious deficiency of statistical data on private short-term capital movements before 1914 will doubtless pose an obstacle to further systematic work in this field, except perhaps in the form of approaches which dispense with the use of such statistics altogether.

[4] Viner, *Studies*, p. 407.

# APPENDIX I

Exchange-Rate Parties of Gold Currencies
in Terms of the U.S. Dollar Before 1914*

| | |
|---|---|
| French franc | $0.193 |
| Belgian franc | 0.193 |
| Swiss franc | 0.193 |
| Dutch guilder | 0.402 |
| Norwegian krone | 0.268 |
| Swedish krone | 0.268 |
| Danish krone | 0.268 |
| British pound | 4.867 |
| German mark | 0.238 |
| Finnish mark | 0.193 |
| Italian lira | 0.193 |
| Russian ruble | 0.515 |
| Austrian-Hungarian crown | 0.203 |
| Japanese yen | 0.499 |
| Roumanian leu | 0.193 |
| Netherlands East Indies guilder | 0.402 |
| Indian rupee | 0.325 |

* Used for converting foreign currency into U.S.
dollars in Table I, Chart 1, and Appendix II.

# APPENDIX II
## Official Foreign-Exchange Holdings By Countries
### (millions of pre-1914 dollars)

| Year (Dec. 31) | Bel-gium | Nor-way | Fin-land | India | Den-mark | Ger-many | Swe-den | Hol-land | Java | Austria-Hun-gary |
|---|---|---|---|---|---|---|---|---|---|---|
| 1880 | 22.4 | 2.8 | 7.4 | 13.6 | 2.6 | 6.0 | 8.0 | | | |
| 1881 | 14.1 | 2.4 | 6.4 | 8.3 | 3.3 | 4.5 | 7.3 | | | |
| 1882 | 18.0 | 2.8 | 5.6 | 11.2 | 2.8 | 1.6 | 6.8 | | | |
| 1883 | 26.1 | 3.2 | 6.4 | 13.6 | 2.8 | 2.5 | 7.1 | | | |
| 1884 | 28.9 | 3.0 | 6.1 | 7.3 | 3.0 | 2.0 | 7.3 | | | |
| 1885 | 28.4 | 2.5 | 5.3 | 15.6 | 2.3 | 6.7 | 6.8 | | | |
| 1886 | 33.0 | 2.7 | 5.4 | 17.0 | 5.0 | 5.6 | 8.3 | | | |
| 1887 | 31.6 | 3.3 | 4.1 | 19.4 | 7.2 | 3.7 | 8.5 | | | |
| 1888 | 28.9 | 4.4 | 4.1 | 10.7 | 4.0 | 3.0 | 12.3 | | | |
| 1889 | 34.0 | 4.2 | 6.0 | 17.5 | 4.1 | 3.0 | 10.9 | 13.0 | | |
| 1890 | 31.7 | 2.7 | 5.4 | 12.7 | 3.1 | 1.7 | 9.3 | 3.3 | | |
| 1891 | 34.7 | 2.7 | 4.5 | 13.6 | 2.7 | 4.7 | 8.1 | 6.8 | 1.8 | |
| 1892 | 37.9 | 3.5 | 4.8 | 7.3 | 3.7 | 3.5 | 7.9 | 9.5 | 1.6 | |
| 1893 | 39.5 | 1.6 | 3.6 | 4.4 | 4.2 | 1.7 | 10.0 | 9.3 | 1.8 | |
| 1894 | 41.7 | 1.7 | 6.3 | 8.3 | 6.3 | 1.9 | 11.1 | 9.8 | 1.2 | |
| 1895 | 41.9 | 2.6 | 9.2 | 11.2 | 4.4 | 2.0 | 12.3 | 6.7 | 1.3 | |
| 1896 | 43.4 | 2.1 | 10.3 | 9.3 | 2.6 | 2.0 | 12.8 | 2.0 | 2.1 | 8.3 |
| 1897 | 50.9 | 5.1 | 11.4 | 8.3 | 3.5 | 3.6 | 15.0 | 2.9 | 3.4 | 7.7 |
| 1898 | 35.9 | 3.8 | 13.0 | 10.2 | 1.3 | 8.6 | 13.9 | 3.0 | 2.8 | 2.7 |
| 1899 | 41.9 | 3.5 | 9.8 | 16.1 | 1.3 | 7.9 | 21.5 | 2.2 | 2.4 | 4.1 |
| 1900 | 50.7 | 2.6 | 9.9 | 20.0 | 1.2 | 19.1 | 22.2 | 4.1 | 2.2 | 12.2 |
| 1901 | 66.5 | 3.3 | 10.8 | 49.7 | 4.6 | 13.5 | 22.1 | 4.4 | 0.5 | 12.2 |
| 1902 | 63.8 | 1.5 | 14.8 | 46.7 | 3.3 | 15.3 | 17.4 | 4.0 | 1.6 | 12.2 |
| 1903 | 63.3 | 2.0 | 15.7 | 66.7 | 2.0 | 12.9 | 14.0 | 2.5 | 2.0 | 12.2 |
| 1904 | 67.0 | 3.3 | 12.7 | 90.6 | 2.4 | 13.1 | 19.0 | 7.2 | 2.7 | 12.2 |
| 1905 | 57.9 | 3.6 | 17.0 | 106.7 | 2.3 | 16.2 | 20.6 | 8.4 | 1.9 | 12.2 |
| 1906 | 63.6 | 5.4 | 18.6 | 94.4 | 1.4 | 20.0 | 23.6 | 2.5 | 0.6 | 12.2 |
| 1907 | 46.7 | 7.5 | 17.0 | 93.0 | 1.9 | 8.5 | 18.3 | 2.3 | 2.3 | 12.2 |
| 1908 | 62.8 | 6.8 | 14.3 | 81.3 | 2.9 | 36.6 | 25.1 | 6.5 | 4.8 | 12.2 |
| 1909 | 58.3 | 7.3 | 20.6 | 147.6 | 3.7 | 44.6 | 26.0 | 7.3 | 5.7 | 12.2 |
| 1910 | 56.4 | 6.8 | 21.9 | 171.9 | 5.1 | 58.6 | 28.5 | 3.0 | 6.5 | 12.2 |
| 1911 | 55.3 | 6.2 | 20.9 | 189.0 | 5.7 | 40.7 | 52.5 | 6.6 | 6.5 | 12.2 |
| 1912 | 71.6 | 6.9 | 17.4 | 135.9 | 7.2 | 25.6 | 36.8 | 6.5 | 6.7 | 12.2 |
| 1913 | 77.7 | 8.9 | 20.9 | 136.4 | 6.2 | 49.6 | 43.4 | 5.5 | 4.7 | 12.2 |

| Year (Dec. 31) | Rou-mania | Italy | Russia | Japan | Philip-pines | France | Chile | Switzer-land | Total |
|---|---|---|---|---|---|---|---|---|---|
| 1880 | | | | | | | | | 62.8 |
| 1881 | | | | | | | | | 46.3 |
| 1882 | | | | | | | | | 48.8 |
| 1883 | | | | | | | | | 61.7 |
| 1884 | | | | | | | | | 57.6 |
| 1885 | | | | | | | | | 67.6 |
| 1886 | | | | | | | | | 77.0 |
| 1887 | | | | | | | | | 77.8 |
| 1888 | | | | | | | | | 67.4 |
| 1889 | | | | | | | | | 92.7 |
| 1890 | | | | | | | | | 69.9 |
| 1891 | | | | | | | | | 79.6 |
| 1892 | | | | | | | | | 79.7 |
| 1893 | | | | | | | | | 76.1 |
| 1894 | | | | | | | | | 88.3 |
| 1895 | | | | | | | | | 91.6 |
| 1896 | 2.7 | | | | | | | | 97.6 |
| 1897 | 2.9 | | | | | | | | 114.7 |
| 1898 | 4.0 | 17.9 | | | | | | | 117.1 |
| 1899 | 2.8 | 19.6 | | | | | | | 133.1 |
| 1900 | 2.0 | 22.4 | | | | | | | 168.6 |
| 1901 | 3.9 | 22.9 | 51.3 | | | | | | 265.7 |
| 1902 | 5.5 | 23.6 | 100.6 | | | | | | 310.3 |
| 1903 | 6.0 | 24.7 | 182.8 | 42.2 | | | | | 449.0 |
| 1904 | 3.9 | 35.8 | 181.8 | 41.6 | 3.0 | | | | 496.3 |
| 1905 | 6.1 | 27.2 | 129.1 | 52.2 | 2.6 | 1.0 | 16.6 | | 481.6 |
| 1906 | 6.7 | 32.3 | 223.8 | 65.9 | 2.3 | 5.3 | 27.7 | | 606.3 |
| 1907 | 7.6 | 29.4 | 159.6 | 79.6 | 3.8 | 16.8 | 29.6 | 5.3 | 541.4 |
| 1908 | 6.5 | 30.2 | 103.0 | 57.0 | 4.3 | 1.9 | 30.6 | 8.6 | 495.4 |
| 1909 | 7.3 | 30.1 | 266.3 | 57.8 | 7.1 | 13.0 | 31.5 | 9.4 | 755.8 |
| 1910 | 9.4 | 34.2 | 298.2 | 67.9 | 9.6 | 9.1 | 35.0 | 11.4 | 845.7 |
| 1911 | 11.9 | 33.9 | 302.3 | 77.8 | 11.4 | 1.9 | 36.3 | 4.7 | 875.8 |
| 1912 | 12.2 | 35.0 | 335.6 | 92.3 | 11.4 | 4.3 | 37.6 | 5.2 | 860.4 |
| 1913 | 10.9 | 38.1 | 306.1 | 115.8 | 11.4 | 3.2 | 39.0 | 8.2 | 898.2 |

# APPENDIX III

## Sources and Composition of Series on Official Foreign-Exchange Holdings

*Belgium.* Comprises foreign balances of National Bank of Belgium, foreign bills held by the Belgium Treasury, and foreign bills held by the *Caisse Générale d'Epargne et de Retraite.* The National Bank's holdings are taken from "La Banque Nationale de Belgique, 1850-1950," *Bulletin d'Information et de Documentation,* September 1950, pp. 117-118. Statistics of the Treasury's holdings were provided by the National Bank of Belgium, and those of the Caisse's holdings were taken from the latter's annual reports.

*Norway.* Represents the Bank of Norway's accounts with foreign correspondents and, from 1887, holdings of foreign bills. There is no separate breakdown for the latter before 1887, but this item was in any case very small until 1905. Statistics were provided by the Bank of Norway.

*Finland.* Comprises Bank of Finland's current accounts abroad and its holdings of foreign bills, foreign bonds, and foreign currency. The figures for 1881-1884 are somewhat less complete than for the other years. Data are taken from *Annuaire Statistique de Finlande,* 1918, pp. 316-317, and from the annual reports of the Bank of Finland for missing years.

*India.* Consists of the Treasury's "Cash Balances" in London from 1880, and the sterling components of the "Gold Standard Reserve" and the "Paper Currency Reserve" from 1900. The figures are actually for March 31 of each year, but for purposes of Charts 1 and 3 and Appendix II are considered to represent those for December 31 of the preceding year. The sources are J. M. Keynes, *Indian Currency and Finance* (London, 1913), p. 128; G. F. Shirras, *Indian Finance and Banking* (London, 1919), pp. 319, 463, and 465; and *Banking and Monetary Statistics of India* (Reserve Bank of India, 1954), pp. 647, 668, 873, and 878. "Cash Balances" in London for the earlier years were derived by subtracting Central Government balances in India from total Central Government balances. (The Indian figures for the years 1880-1898 used in Appendix II and Chart 1 are actually incorrect and should not have been included. After Chart 1 had been drawn, I recognized that I had carelessly overlooked the fact that during those years the Indian rupee was fluctuating in terms of gold and that I should not have converted the rupee amount of the Indian Government's "Cash Balances" abroad into dollars on the basis of the fixed gold parity that was established in 1899. This error on my part does not, however, significantly affect the *aggregate* of official foreign-exchange holdings shown in Chart 1 and Appendix II for these earlier years.)

*Denmark*. Consists of the National Bank of Denmark's holdings of foreign bills and the amounts due the Bank from foreign correspondents. Figures were supplied by the National Bank of Denmark. The Bank also held, at least in the later years of the period, some foreign bonds, but the complete series is not available.

*Germany*. Series includes the Reichsbank's holdings of foreign bills and the amounts due it from foreign correspondents. The data are taken from *Die Reichsbank, 1876-1910* (Berlin, 1910), pp. 158-160; and *Die Reichsbank, 1901-1925* (Berlin, 1925), Vol. II, pp. 76-77.

*Sweden*. Comprises the Bank of Sweden's current accounts abroad and its holdings of foreign bills and foreign bonds, as well as the foreign-exchange holdings of the National Debt Office. The figures for the Bank of Sweden were obtained from *Sveriges Riksbank, 1668-1924*, Vol. V (Stockholm, 1931), pp. 26-31. The data for the National Debt Office were provided by the Bank of Sweden.

*Netherlands*. Consists of the foreign-bill holdings of the Netherlands Bank, which made the data available to me.

*Java*. Represents "Bills payable outside the Netherlands East Indies" held by the Java Bank. The figures are taken from L. D. Bree, *Gedenkboek van De Javasche Bank* (Weltevreden, 1928), Vol. II, p. 401, and statistical appendix. The figures are for March 31, but for purposes of Chart 1 and Appendix II are considered to represent those for December 31 of the preceding year.

*Austria-Hungary*. Consists of the published foreign-bill holdings of the Austro-Hungarian Bank, which made the data available to me from its balance sheets.

*Roumania*. Consists of the foreign-bill holdings of the National Bank of Roumania. Data were taken from the annual reports of the Bank.

*Italy*. Comprises the total of foreign bills (including Treasury bills) and current accounts abroad held by the Bank of Italy, the Bank of Naples, and the Bank of Sicily. Data were provided by the Bank of Italy. (The foreign-exchange holdings of the Italian Treasury used in Chart 3, but not included in Chart 1 or Appendix II, were also provided by the Bank of Italy).

*Russia.* Consists of balances held abroad by the State Bank of Russia and the Russian Government. The data for the Bank's foreign balances for 1901 to 1906 were taken from A. Z. Arnold, *Banks, Credits, and Money in Soviet Russia* (New York, 1937), p. 16, who draws upon the Bank's pre-1914 balance sheets. (This item was reported under the heading of "Gold held abroad.") The data for the foreign balances of the Russian Treasury from 1901 to 1906, were made available by Dr. Olga Crisp. For 1907 to 1912, I used the figures for the combined foreign balances of the State Bank and the Russian Treasury given in M. W. Bernatzky, "Monetary Policy of the Russian Government During the War," in A. M. Michelson, P. N. Apostol, and M. W. Bernatzky, *Russian Public Finance During the War* (New Haven, 1928), p. 352. The combined figure for 1913 was taken from V. A. Mukoseyev, "Money and Credit," in *Russia: Its Trade and Commerce*, ed. by A. Raffalovich (London, 1918), pp. 398-399. All of the Russian data were actually reported for January 1, but I have used them to represent the figures for December 31 of the preceding year.

*Japan.* Consists of the holdings of foreign exchange, foreign government bonds, and foreign currency of the Yokohama Specie Bank. The figures were provided by the Bank of Japan.

*Philippines.* Consists of the U.S. dollar portion of the Gold Standard Fund, as reported in the *Annual Report of the Treasurer of the Philippines* from 1904 to 1911. Since comparable figures were not available for 1912 and 1913, I used the 1911 figure for these two years also.

*France.* Consists of the foreign bills held by the Bank of France. The series is based upon data provided by the Bank of France. (The Bank also held 75 million francs, or $14.5 million, of English Treasury bills at the end of 1890 as the result of a loan in gold to the Bank of England in November 1890, these holdings being liquidated in February 1891. This amount is not shown in Chart 1 or Appendix II.)

*Chile.* Consists of the holdings of the Chilean Government's conversion funds in foreign banks, as reported, on the basis of official statistics in terms of sterling, in F. W. Fetter, *Monetary Inflation in Chile* (Princeton, 1931), p. 116. In private correspondence Professor Fetter has informed me that it was certainly his impression that this reserve was held in the form of a bank deposit and not in the form of physical gold; and I have accepted his judgment for purposes of Chart 1 and Appendix II. According to G. Subercaseaux, *Monetary and Banking Policy of Chile* (Oxford, 1922), pp. 144-145, however, these holdings were in the form of gold.

*Switzerland.* Comprises the item "devises" (foreign exchange) on the balance sheet of the National Bank of Switzerland, as reported in the Bank's *Annual Report* for 1956, p. 58. According to an explanatory note attached thereto, this item in 1907 and 1908 consisted only of foreign bills, and from 1909-1913 included only foreign bills and sight deposits abroad.

# PUBLICATIONS OF THE
# INTERNATIONAL FINANCE SECTION

The International Finance Section publishes at irregular intervals papers in three series: ESSAYS IN INTERNATIONAL FINANCE, PRINCETON STUDIES IN INTERNATIONAL FINANCE, and SPECIAL PAPERS IN INTERNATIONAL ECONOMICS. All three of these may be ordered directly from the Section.

Single copies of the ESSAYS are distributed without charge to all interested persons, both here and abroad. Additional copies of any one issue may be obtained from the Section at a charge of $0.25 a copy, payable in advance. Institutions of education or research will be supplied up to five copies free of charge.

For the STUDIES and SPECIAL PAPERS there will be a charge of $1.00 a copy. This charge will be waived on single copies requested by persons residing abroad and on copies (up to five) distributed to college and university libraries here and abroad.

Standing requests to receive new ESSAYS as they are issued and notices of the publication of new STUDIES and SPECIAL PAPERS will be honored. Because of frequent changes of address and the resulting waste, students will not be placed on the permanent mailing list.

The following is a complete list of the publications of the International Finance Section. The issues of the three series that are still available from the Section are marked by asterisks. Those marked by daggers are out of stock at the International Finance Section but may be obtained from University Microfilms, Inc., 313 N. First Street, Ann Arbor, Michigan.

## ESSAYS IN INTERNATIONAL FINANCE

† 1. Friedrich A. Lutz, International Monetary Mechanisms: The Keynes and White Proposals. (July 1943)

† 2. Frank D. Graham, Fundamentals of International Monetary Policy. (Autumn 1943)

† 3. Richard A. Lester, International Aspects of Wartime Monetary Experience. (Aug. 1944)

† 4. Ragnar Nurkse, Conditions of International Monetary Equilibrium. (Spring 1945)

† 5. Howard S. Ellis, Bilateralism and the Future of International Trade. (Summer 1945)

† 6. Arthur I. Bloomfield, The British Balance-of-Payments Problem. (Autumn 1945)

† 7. Frank A. Southard, Jr., Some European Currency and Exchange Experiences. (Summer 1946)

† 8. Miroslav A. Kriz, Postwar International Lending. (Spring 1947)

† 9. Friedrich A. Lutz, The Marshall Plan and European Economic Policy. (Spring 1948)

†10. Frank D. Graham, The Cause and Cure of "Dollar Shortage." (Jan. 1949)

†11. Horst Mendershausen, Dollar Shortage and Oil Surplus in 1949-1950. (Nov. 1950)

†12. Sir Arthur Salter, Foreign Investment. (Feb. 1951)

†13. Sir Roy Harrod, The Pound Sterling. (Feb. 1952)

†14. S. Herbert Frankel, Some Conceptual Aspects of International Economic Development of Underdeveloped Territories. (May 1952)

†15. Miroslav A. Kriz, The Price of Gold. (July 1952)

†16. William Diebold, Jr., The End of the I.T.O. (Oct. 1952)

†17. Sir Douglas Copland, Problems of the Sterling Area: With Special Reference to Australia. (Sept. 1953)

†18. Raymond F. Mikesell, The Emerging Pattern of International Payments. (April 1954)

†19. D. Gale Johnson, Agricultural Price Policy and International Trade. (June 1954)

†20. Ida Greaves, "The Colonial Sterling Balances." (Sept. 1954)

†21. Raymond Vernon, America's Foreign Trade Policy and the GATT. (Oct. 1954)

†22. Roger Auboin, The Bank for International Settlements, 1930-1955. (May 1955)

†23. Wytze Gorter, United States Merchant Marine Policies: Some International Implications. (June 1955)

†24. Thomas C. Schelling, International Cost-Sharing Arrangements. (Sept. 1955)

†25. James E. Meade, The Belgium-Luxembourg Economic Union, 1921-1939. (March 1956)

†26. Samuel I. Katz, Two Approaches to the Exchange-Rate Problem: The United Kingdom and Canada. (Aug. 1956)

†27. A. R. Conan, The Changing Pattern of International Investment in Selected Sterling Countries. (Dec. 1956)

†28. Fred H. Klopstock, The International Status of the Dollar. (May 1957)

†29. Raymond Vernon, Trade Policy in Crisis. (March 1958)

†30. Sir Roy Harrod, The Pound Sterling, 1951-1958. (Aug. 1958)

†31. Randall Hinshaw, Toward European Convertibility. (Nov. 1958)

†32. Francis H. Schott, The Evolution of Latin American Exchange-Rate Policies since World War II. (Jan. 1959)

†33. Alec Cairncross, The International Bank for Reconstruction and Development. (March 1959)

†34. Miroslav A. Kriz, Gold in World Monetary Affairs Today. (June 1959)

†35. Sir Donald MacDougall, The Dollar Problem: A Reappraisal. (Nov. 1960)

†36. Brian Tew, The International Monetary Fund: Its Present Role and Future Prospects. (March 1961)

*37. Samuel I. Katz, Sterling Speculation and European Convertibility: 1955-1958. (Oct. 1961)
*38. Boris C. Swerling, Current Issues in Commodity Policy. (June 1962)
*39. Pieter Lieftinck, Recent Trends in International Monetary Policies. (Sept. 1962)
*40. Jerome L. Stein, The Nature and Efficiency of the Foreign Exchange Market. (Oct. 1962)
*41. Friedrich A. Lutz, The Problem of International Liquidity and the Multiple-Currency Standard. (March 1963)
*42. Sir Dennis Robertson, A Memorandum Submitted to the Canadian Royal Commission on Banking and Finance. (May 1963)

## PRINCETON STUDIES IN INTERNATIONAL FINANCE

† 1. Friedrich A. and Vera C. Lutz, Monetary and Foreign Exchange Policy in Italy. (Jan. 1950)
† 2. Eugene A. Schlesinger, Multiple Exchange Rates and Economic Development. (May 1952)
† 3. Arthur I. Bloomfield, Speculative and Flight Movements of Capital in Postwar International Finance. (Feb. 1954)
† 4. Merlyn N. Trued and Raymond F. Mikesell, Postwar Bilateral Payments Agreements. (April 1955)
† 5. Derek Curtis Bok, The First Three Years of the Schuman Plan. (Dec. 1955)
† 6. James E. Meade, Negotiations for Benelux: An Annotated Chronicle, 1943-1956. (March 1957)
† 7. H. H. Liesner, The Import Dependence of Britain and Western Germany: A Comparative Study. (Dec. 1957)
† 8. Raymond F. Mikesell and Jack N. Behrman, Financing Free World Trade with the Sino-Soviet Bloc. (Sept. 1958)
* 9. Marina von Neumann Whitman, The United States Investment Guaranty Program and Private Foreign Investment. (Dec. 1959)
*10. Peter B. Kenen, Reserve-Asset Preferences of Central Banks and Stability of the Gold-Exchange Standard. (Feb. 1963)
*11. Arthur I. Bloomfield, Short-Term Capital Movements under the Pre-1914 Gold Standard. (June 1963)

## SPECIAL PAPERS IN INTERNATIONAL ECONOMICS

* 1. Gottfried Haberler, A Survey of International Trade Theory. (revised edition, July 1961)
† 2. Oskar Morgenstern, The Validity of International Gold Movement Statistics. (Nov. 1955)
* 3. Fritz Machlup, Plans for Reform of the International Monetary System. (Aug. 1962)
* 4. Egon Sohmen, International Monetary Problems and the Foreign Exchanges. (April 1963)